*Safely Detox From Alcohol and Drugs at Home - How to Stop Drinking and Beat Addiction*

*by Taite Adams*

# Copyright


Rapid Response Press
1730 Lighthouse Terr S., Suite 12
So. Pasadena, FL 33707
www.rapidresponsepress.com
Ordering Information:
Quantity sales. Special discounts are available on quantity purchases by corporations, associations, and others. For details, contact the publisher at the address above.
Orders by U.S. trade bookstores and wholesalers. Please contact Rapid Response Press: Tel: (866) 983-3025; Fax: (855) 877-4736 or visit www.rapidresponsepress.com.
Printed in the United States of America
Publisher's Cataloging-in-Publication data
Adams, Taite.
A title of a book : a subtitle of the same book / Taite Adams.
p. cm.
ISBN 978-0-9889875-3-1
1. The main category of the book —Health —Other category. 2. Another subject category —Mind and Body. 3. More categories — Recovery.

Second Edition
==================

## Limit of Liability/Disclaimer of Warranty



For general information on our other products and services or for technical support please contact Rapid Response Press - 1730 Lighthouse Terr., Suite 12; So. Pasadena, FL 33707

================

## Disclaimer



=================

## Medical Disclaimer

The information contained in this book is not intended to serve as a replacement for professional medical advice. Any use of the information in this book is at the reader's discretion. The author and publisher specifically disclaim any and all liability arising directly or indirectly from the use or application of any information contained in this book. A health care professional should be consulted regarding your specific situation.

To my son - I am so proud of you and pray to God you never need this book;
To Mom - For your continued love and undying support;
To my love - Each day with you is another miracle. I am looking forward to many more.

# Contents

# Preface

This Guide on how to detox from alcohol and drugs at home was born out of necessity, in a sense. While this is something that countless people attempt, most times in vain, there is really no instruction book of its sort available and no doubt the need is there. While going "cold turkey" off of certain substances and sweating it out on your couch won't win Idea of the Year, the fact remains that people are doing it and relying on conflicting information that they find on online message boards or Yahoo Answers to get them through the experience, often resulting in unplanned visits from the paramedics or needless suffering.

There are ways to detox from alcohol and withdraw from drugs in the privacy of your own home IF you meet certain criteria and IF you make the proper preparations. These are all covered in this book. Yes, I do have experience detoxing from drugs and alcohol and from doing so without professional help. While not pleasant, it wasn't life threatening (any of the times) and my experiences were able to contribute to the content of this guide. Not to mention the fact that I belong to a community of people in which many have also had these experiences and have been more than willing (and eager at times) to share them with me.

The control freak in the addict and alcoholic does not want to "check in" someplace or relinquish their freedom. I get that. We also want to know what may be in store for us if we decide to "do this". That is also perfectly understandable. I have attempted to outline in this Guide what you need to do in order to lay out a solid detox plan for yourself, set up a tapering schedule if it applies, manage cravings and then deal with the withdrawal symptoms of your particular drug (or alcohol). Please note that everyone's experience is different, however, and yours likely will vary. Also, it's crucial that you have support in place and don't attempt this at home unless you meet the basic criteria laid out in this book. Even then, understand that you are doing this at your own risk and this a choice that you alone can make. Otherwise, here is how to detox from drugs and alcohol at home. Best of luck to you.

# How to Detox at Home

*When you're drowning, you don't say 'I would be incredibly pleased if someone would have the foresight to notice me drowning and come and help me,' you just scream. -John Lennon*

First and foremost, what is "detox"? A "toxin" is anything that impedes normal functions of the body, or causes stagnation, congestion or dis-ease. What keeps things from being toxic? The circulatory, lymph system, colon, liver, urinary system, etc. 'Blockage' of any of these systems - for example, by making them work too hard, or overloading them - can ultimately result in toxins accumulating in the body. "Detoxification" or 'detox' refers to the period of time it takes for the 'active' toxins to leave the body -- as little as a week or as long as several months.

Who in their right mind would want to detox from any substance at home? Well, if you're reading this book, chances are that you or a loved one have not been in the right frame of mind for quite some time. Hence the dilemma, right? Yes, there are a plethora of professional detox facilities that you can go to for drug and alcohol treatment and many local hospitals are now in the detox business as well. Perhaps you've gone this route in the past and it was a wasted effort (pun intended). There are a lot of reasons why you shouldn't detox at home and we'll get to those coming up. However, most of the people that would buy a book of this sort are looking to carry out this exercise and here are some of the reasons that you may have for doing so:

**Access** - Getting into detox facilities isn't as easy as it once was, particularly the ones that are paid for with public funds. It's no longer as simple as having your friends drive you up to the front doors and pushing you out of the back seat of the car. There are actually waiting lists for these places now. I don't know about you but, when I'm ready to "get clean", I'd prefer not to have to take a number and get in line.

Many people are continually breaking the law to obtain their substances of choice and are looking to stop doing this as well. Being unable to get into detox presents a huge Catch 22. Now, if you are willing to pay for a private facility, of course the doors will swing wide open for you. This presents another access issue.

**Privacy** - Many people mired in the depths of their addiction seem to think that no one knows what's going on with them and it's a big "secret". This may be true in a few rare cases. So, if you are worried about privacy and other people finding out, either now or in the future, this may be a reason to tough it out at home. There will be no record of your detox stay and you can start your life fresh in the comfort and privacy of your own home.

**Time** - Family and work obligations often come in front of our own personal well-being. The thought of taking time off to actually check into an inpatient facility to detox from drugs and alcohol is simply out of the question for some as they have children or job obligations. I would stress that you take a very close look at this one because, home or away, detox is never pleasant and you will be "useful" to no one during this process. You may be physically present and, if that is all that is required of your job, fantastic. The detox process is different for everyone though and you shouldn't expect to be productive in any way, shape or form either personally or professionally so arrangements should be made to accommodate this.

# Home Detox Considerations

The type of withdrawals, their intensity, the duration, and the preparations necessary for detox are going to depend entirely on the type of drug being abused as well as the scale of abuse. Certain drugs most definitely have a more intense and prolonged detoxification period, and some can even be dangerous or life-threatening. There are many things to consider before undertaking a home detox so that you are successful, comfortable and safe.

## Why Are You Stopping?

Don't gloss over this - it's huge. In fact, it's a whole other book but unless you have some understanding of why you are doing this, this is going to be wasted time (there's that pun again). While it's ok to want to stop using drugs and alcohol for other people, you also have to want to stop doing so for your own sake. If legal, financial, work and family consequences are piling up as a result of your addiction, how does this make you feel? If these things are making you tired of using drugs and alcohol, you're probably in the right place.

If you are still not sure about this, list out the positive and negative aspects of your drug and/or alcohol use. Seriously, get out a piece of paper and a pen. What are these things bringing to your life? Be honest, this list is only for your benefit and doesn't need to be shared with anyone else. For many, in the beginning, drugs made them feel good. However, that is just a "chased" feeling in the end and just not fun anymore. In the end, most people can see that drugs and alcohol, when used to excess, actually took them away from the social scene, left them isolated, were damaging their health, hurt family and friends, were illegal or caused them to do things that were illegal, diminished their self-image and had many more negative aspects than positive. Be courageous and make your list before you go any further.

## What Drugs Are You Using?

Stopping the addictive use of any substance is going to have some affects; it doesn't matter if it's over-the-counter Benadryl or Heroin. However, there is a huge difference in the type of physical and psychological withdrawal that will occur when you stop taking them and the duration of those symptoms. Many addicts don't take just one thing either. They may take opiates during the day and Benzos at night to sleep. Or they may drink during the day and take sedatives at night. So, make a list of all of the drugs (including alcohol) that you are taking on a daily basis and the quantities. Again, be honest here. And, again, this isn't a mental list - find that pen! This is your detox and you are going to be running the show (mostly). If you want to be successful, you can't downplay or gloss over anything.

There is ongoing debate as to whether withdrawal from certain drugs is classified as "physical" or merely psychological. It's widely agreed that physical symptoms can be expected when you detox from: opiates (heroin, methadone, oxycodone), benzodiazepines (valium, ativan), barbiturates (seconal, fioricet) and alcohol. It was thought for many years that marijuana and amphetamines were not addictive but that you would simply experience mental craving after stopping their use. (This is nothing to shake a stick at, by the way). These notions are being re-examined and will be discussed more in depth in each section. However, if stopping a substance results in you being unable to concentrate or sleep, chances are there will be some physical consequences. Additionally, cocaine withdrawal is now thought to have a physical component to it as well as the intense psychological craving.

Again, get your list of substances and usage levels done so that you know what you are going to be dealing with and can be prepared based on the withdrawal symptoms and preparations listed for each substance listed later on.

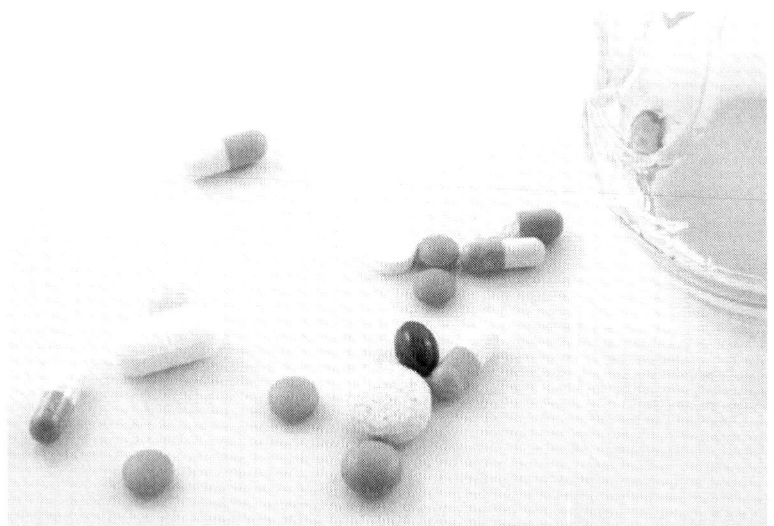

## Who is Your Supplier?

Every good drug addict has a supplier and back-up, or ten. Don't wait until after you go through detox to consider this. How were you obtaining your drugs on a regular basis and what is your plan of action with regards to that source(s) in the future? This could very well be the family doctor or a pain management doctor if you are addicted to pain meds or Benzos. Depending on the circumstances, and your willingness, you could absolutely try to enlist this professional as an "ally" in your detoxification procedure. Many of the recommendations in this book will call for a prescription, only if you can get one. So, if you have an understanding physician in your corner, this would be the time to set up an appointment and let them know your plans and your humble request for help.

If you obtained your drugs illegally, consider that you are going to have to break ties with these contacts. You will need to delete them from your phone, block the numbers, do whatever you need to do. The temptations and cravings will be very strong at times and this is one of the reasons why some self-examination is important before starting the process. Know why you are doing this and be fully committed. Don't give yourself a bunch of "outs" and escape routes if you want to be successful. This is an extremely difficult endeavor to do alone.

## Get Some Support

*"Asking for help does not mean that we are weak or incompetent. It usually indicates an advanced level of honesty and intelligence." -Jim Rohn*

For some, the whole idea of doing a home detox means that they want to do this "alone" and have no one know about it. This is both difficult and dangerous. It's difficult because we can be our own worst enemies and because addiction is such a powerful disease that cravings are tough to combat when all alone. It's dangerous because of the physical, and sometimes psychological, component to detox and withdrawal. When not in a medically supervised setting, detox can be scary at times and there may be rare instances where medical intervention is necessary. If you don't have someone that is checking up on you and monitoring your progress, you may not be in the proper state to make that call.

If possible, enlist a family member or friend to help you through the most difficult days of this process. A person who also has alcohol or drug-related problems would not be a good candidate for this role. Your support person's availability to help you and be present for you, ideally, most of the time during the difficult days would be. Depending on what substance you are withdrawing from, this will vary on which days the symptoms start to how long they last. Read the relevant section of the book for guidance.

A support person can be invaluable in reminding us of why it is that we're doing this in the first place. Believe me, it's easy to forget when the only thing in the forefront of your mind is getting the discomfort to stop in the quickest way possible. If you think that "no one knows" about your problem, you're likely mistaken. It may be worth it to put yourself out there to a trusted friend, family member, or two and experience the relief that comes when you have someone else on your side and rooting for your success. If "everyone knows", there's probably a family member or old friend out there that would love to see you get clean and would be there for you if you asked.

## Health and Safety Considerations

Home detoxification from drugs and alcohol can be achieved under a lot of circumstances, but not all. There is danger involved and it is exacerbated substantially by other physical and psychiatric disorders. Complications from or by other factors may require that you be treated in an inpatient facility for your safety. Some conditions that are of concern would be: unstable diabetes, severe hypertension and severe liver disease. These sorts of conditions would adversely affect the course of withdrawal and, conversely, withdrawal can aggravate these illnesses themselves.

In addition, the presence of unstable psychiatric illness can complicate the management of withdrawal. There may be difficulty in complying with medication regimes and a psychiatric disorder can also intensify some symptoms of withdrawal such as confusion and agitation. A lot of times, alcohol and drugs are used to ease or relieve the symptoms of the psychiatric disorder. When the use stops, the original psychiatric symptoms that were suppressed and acute withdrawal can come forth simultaneously and this needs to be managed in a controlled, professional setting.

HELP!!

## Have a Detox Plan

*"It's not the load that breaks you down; it's the way you carry it."* -Lena Horne

Obviously you've thought about this and are doing some research. These are the sorts of people that put searches in Google and buy books on these things. Good move. Aside from that great first step though, this is a general outline of the plan that you need to put together. More details can be found in the sections of the book for each substance that you will be detoxing from. Yes, you can detox from more than one substance at a time. Don't prolong the misery if you don't have to. Here's the Home Detox Plan:

- Take a look at yourself and why you are stopping (a little self examination exercise)
- Make a List of all of the substances that you are using and quantities
- Call for a Doctor's Appointment if you are able
- Clear your Calendar (try for 2 weeks) - no work or other heavy obligations
- Get some support - Find family or friends that can help you through this
- Put your detox plan together based on your particular substance (see relevant book chapter(s) for this)
- Get things to keep you occupied and entertained - books, movies, etc.
- Begin Detox process
- Keep a detox calendar and diary/journal to track your progress
- Don't use any more drugs or alcohol or switch to something "new".
- Consider a support group afterwards (and even during if you are able to get out).

## To Taper or Not

If you've done some research online, you may have run across some groups that recommend "tapering" off your drug of choice before stopping completely. There are different schools of thought to this and, frankly, logic doesn't always come into play when it comes to talking about addiction and addictive behavior. Yes, it all sounds well and good in theory but how does it work in practice? Not always very well.

Say you are taking 30 painkillers a day (opiates) and someone recommends that you start tapering off and go to 25 or 20 a day. That may be easier said than done, especially if you have those other 5 or 10 in your possession. Regardless of your desire to "quit" or not, this is not an easy proposition and some are more successful with this than others. If you feel that you can trust someone else with your substances (many can't) and can have them rationed out to you, this may work. Otherwise, the craving may still get the best of you and you go straight to a source for more anyway. If you do decide to try tapering, here are some "**Hard Rules for Tapering**" that you will need to stick to:

1. Line up a tough trusted friend, spouse or significant other who will be in charge of your meds and will dole them out to you. This person will have to hold the line no matter how much you whine and try to manipulate.
2. Follow a set schedule. The schedule should be written out and turned over to the person administering the meds.
3. Approach the tapering from a clinical point of view (yes, I know this is difficult).
4. The heavier doses should be first thing in the morning and last of the evening
5. Do not attempt to delay a dosing time and hold off. This will cause a rebound effect that you don't want - ie - you will crave more.

6. Before starting your schedule, count up the exact number of pills you'll require from start to finish...and FLUSH all extraneous pills
7. Before starting your schedule, go to every hiding spot you have and discard those pills. Check jacket pockets, glove compartments, underwear drawers, shoes, handbags, etc. You get the idea. A nasty surprise after you've finished your taper is not something you want to encounter.
8. Hold nothing back "just in case". That's a reservation and it will do you in.
9. Do not rush the taper. Don't get brave. Brave is often foolish and looking for that instant gratification of instant "clean." It won't work.
10. No yo-yo-ing (spiking). An extra pill will interrupt your process and reset your progress. This is highly counter-productive. The goal is to titrate steadily downward.
11. No chewing or snorting. Take them the old fashioned way...with a glass of water and swallow.
12. Cut off all connections; that dealer, that doctor, that pharmacy...whomever. They no longer exist for you. Shut the door firmly. Delete all numbers from your phone.
13. Have no expectation that this will be a comfortable process. Accept it for what it is...a rite of passage to freedom.

One instance where tapering is recommended a lot is in the case of Benzos, because the detox and withdrawal from them is quite severe, dangerous and prolonged. The thought is that if you can get your dosage of these down as much as possible before going off of them completely (see the Benzos Detox Chapter on this), the better off you'll be. Tapering is also used when one is attempting to get free of Methadone, which is another dangerous drug to stop "cold turkey". Clinics will taper patients for a long time before releasing them. Otherwise, methadone withdrawal is also severe and very prolonged.

If you are in one of these situations where tapering may be of benefit to you, consult your physician before starting. Even where other drugs are used in the detox process, they are tapered so as not to cause an additional dependence situation. Otherwise, keep in mind that addiction is a very powerful disease and tapering, by itself, is oftentimes easier said than done.

## Some Tips on Dealing With Cravings

Cravings are urges to drink or use drugs. These urges are a normal part of any addiction and are common-place during withdrawal. They can also pop up months or even years after you stop using drugs or drinking. Here are some important things to remember about cravings and some ways to deal with them.

**What You Should Know About Cravings:**

- They are not caused by a lack of willpower or motivation. It doesn't mean that you are doing something wrong or failing to do something right.
- Cravings don't mean that your detox and withdrawal aren't working.
- Cravings pass. These urges are not constant and are only severe for a very short period of time before they settle down to a more controllable level.
- Cravings can be triggered by physical or psychological discomfort. Managing these can help manage the onset and severity of cravings.

**Things You Can Do to Manage Cravings:**

- Remind yourself that cravings are "temporary". In fact, if the urge to use is very strong, simply put the decision off for an hour and the feelings will likely subside.
- Identify cues or "triggers" that may have brought on the cravings. They could people, places or things that remind you of using. Re-direct your mental energy towards ways in which you can avoid these same triggers in the future.
- Remind yourself of why you stopped taking the drug in the first place. This would be the time to re-list the negative effects that the drug and/or alcohol use had on your life and also list the positive things that you stand to gain by staying clean.

- Call on others for help. This is where a Support Network comes in, supportive family members and friends that support your recovery.
- Use your spirituality to get through cravings. Prayer and meditation can help calm the mind and bring focus back into what you have achieved so far and what lies ahead in your recovery.

Now that we've covered some basic things to know about detoxing at home, tapering and managing cravings, let's get into what you need to do to manage the detox and withdrawals from your particular drug of choice, or from alcohol.

## Home Alcohol Detox

*Courage is the price that life exacts for granting peace. -Amelia Earhart*

Many people don't take alcohol detox seriously enough for several reasons. It's a "legal substance" so to speak, as compared to some of the other drugs discussed in this book, it's commonly used and the withdrawal dangers aren't widely known. Alcohol withdrawal symptoms generally occur after stopping, or a significant reduction of prolonged alcohol intake. This generally means drinking 80 grams (8 drinks) or more a day on a regular basis.

Heavy, prolonged drinking, particularly daily drinking, disrupts the brains neurotransmitters. For instance, alcohol initially enhances the effect of GABA, the neurotransmitter that gives the feeling of calm and relaxation. But chronic alcohol consumption will eventually suppress GABA activity so that more and more is required for this effect, known as "tolerance". Chronic alcohol consumption also suppresses the activity of glutamate, which produces feelings of excitability. To function properly, the glutamate system has to overcompensate and work harder than it would in non-drinkers.

When heavy drinkers stop drinking, the neurotransmitters that were suppressed by their drinking rebound, resulting in what's called brain hyperexcitability. This produces the effects of - anxiety, irritability, agitation, tremors, seizures, and possibly DTs. This is the short list and not something to take lightly. If any of the following apply to you, please consider a professionally supervised inpatient detox:

- Past history of severe withdrawal - If you have had severe withdrawal symptoms in the past, chances are that you will have them again.
- Presence of other illness, injury or recent surgery. This increases the likelihood of severe withdrawals.

- Use of other psychotropic drugs - Simultaneous use of alcohol and other CNS depressants leads to additive, or enhanced, effects. This needs to be managed when you take away the alcohol.

Remember the list of contraindicated physical and psychological conditions for a home detox? These are particularly important to consider in the case of alcohol detox because, even with the healthiest person otherwise, there are dangers involved. That being said, here is what you can expect.

## What to Expect When You Stop Drinking

Detoxing from alcohol is a two-phase process. The first phase begins within 6-24 hours of the last drink of alcohol and can last up to 5-7 days. It's during this period that the person could experience some dangerous withdrawal symptoms that may require medical attention and should be monitored very closely should you decide to do this at home. The second, and longer, phase of alcohol detox occurs over many months as the brain slowly begins to resume normal functioning. This is when sleep patterns are re-established and emotions are regulated. The first phase of alcohol detox symptoms may include the following:

**Mild to Moderate Physical Withdrawal Symptoms**

- Nausea
- Shakiness
- Insomnia
- Loss of appetite
- Headaches
- Clammy skin
- Sweating
- Enlarged or dilated pupils
- Abnormal movements

**Psychological Alcohol Withdrawal Symptoms**

- Anxiety
- Depression
- Nervousness
- Irritability
- Difficulty thinking clearly
- Nightmares
- Fatigue

## Severe Alcohol Withdrawal Symptoms

- Convulsions
- Seizures
- Hallucinations
- Delirium Tremens (DTs)
- Heart Failure
- Muscle tremors
- Extreme confusion
- Black outs
- High fever
- Agitation

Alcohol withdrawal symptoms usually appear within 12 hours of the last drink and the symptoms can peak within 48 to 72 hours. These symptoms can continue for as long as a week or more. 95% of alcohol dependent people who quit drinking suffer from mild to moderate withdrawal symptoms and do not require hospitalization. This does not mean, however, that they would not benefit from a detox facility or from prescription medication to help ease the withdrawal symptoms. Nearly all of them certainly would. The other 5% suffer symptoms so severe that they require hospitalization and medical supervision throughout the process. If you are planning to go through alcohol detox at home, you still have some planning to do.

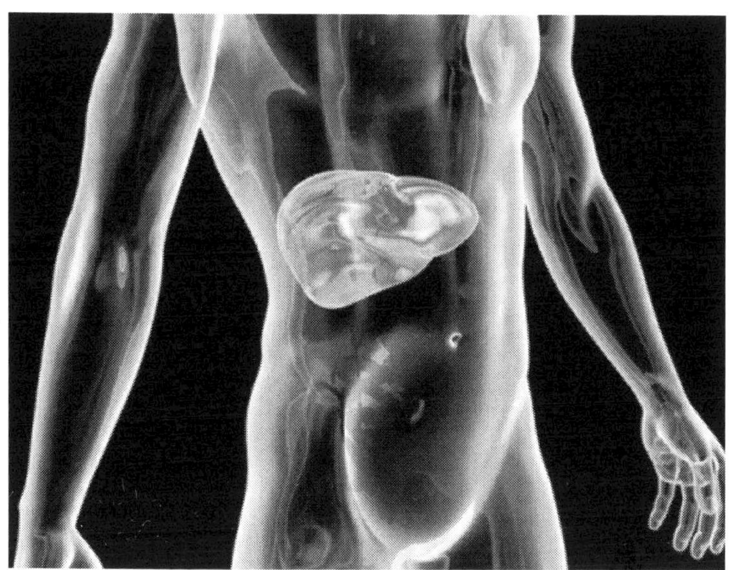

## Preparation for Detoxing From Alcohol at Home

*Everything has its wonders, even darkness and silence, and I learn, whatever state I may be in, therein to be content. -Helen Keller*

If you are planning to detox from alcohol at home, be sure to review the general home detox guide in the first chapter that applies to all home detox procedures. Aside from that, you'll need to make some special preparations with respect to detoxing from alcohol at home.

### Prepare the Environment

One of the reasons that you are likely choosing to do this at home instead of in an institution is "comfort". If so, be sure to have everything on hand to make your stay as comfortable, and safe, as possible. The alcohol withdrawal and detox doesn't last as long as some others but don't expect to be going out on the town during the process. You will be home for the duration so have something to keep yourself busy, whether it be books, movies, games, etc. Also, get rid of all of the alcohol in the home. No joke. There is no "saving some for a special occasion" or "just in case". If you've gone through the exercise in which you address "Why you are doing this", there shouldn't be much resistance here. Just get rid of it - toss it or give it away immediately. Trust me - you will not be able to resist the temptation once the withdrawal symptoms set in.

STOP

## Support

Did you line up a family member or friend to come and stay with you? If not, do so now. This needs to happen from Day 1, particularly with alcohol detox. Probably after Day 3, you will be in the clear and they can just check on you, but this will vary on a case by case basis.

In addition, try to get an appointment with your family physician and request a prescription for a long-acting benzo such as Valium or Librium. Let your physician know what you are trying to do and that you simply want to take a reducing dose of this medication over the course of several days to lessen the withdrawal symptoms. Your doctor will help with proper dosage. However, if you already have Valium or Librium on hand (don't use other Benzos - they're not the same), this is simply an approximation (using Valium) or example for your reference only:

Day 1: 10mg 4 times a day
Day 2: 10 mg 4 times a day
Day 3: 5 mg 4 times a day
Day 4: 5 mg 4 times a day
Day 5: 5 mg 4 times a day
Day 6: 5 mg morning

Aside from a long-acting Benzo (above), these are other prescription medications that are sometimes helpful for mild to moderate withdrawal symptoms:

- **Beta-Blockers** - Such as Propanalol (Inderal) or Atenolol (Tenormin); these are used to slow the heart rate and reduce tremors. These may also help to reduce cravings.

- **Anti-Seizure** - Such as Carbamazepine (Tegretol) or divalproex sodium (Depakote); these anti-seizure agents are usually used together with the Benzos and are not found to be as effective by themselves.

If you are unable to get prescription medication to ease the symptoms, you can still find some comfort with supplements, vitamins and diet.

Here are some over-the-counter medications that you'll want to pick up and their uses:

- **Imodium (Loperamide)** - This is a must-have. It can help with the diarrhea that is likely to come and the gastrointestinal symptoms. Also, it is structurally similar to Demerol and can ease the overall harshness of the detox.
- **Calcium Carbonate (Tums)** - 1 to 2 tablets every 8 hours for abdominal pain and indigestion.
- **OTC Pain Reliever** such as Tylenol, Aleve, Aspirin or Ibuprofen for headache.

As for vitamins and supplements, here are the things that you'll want to consider picking up if your budget allows (you had money for alcohol, didn't you?). Simply stick with the recommended dosages for all of these:

- Vitamin B
- Vitamin C
- L-Glutamine
- Magnesium
- Thiamin
- Niacin
- Milk Thistle (helps with liver repair)
- Melatonin for sleep

## Diet

While there may be periods of time where you have no appetite or are unable to keep anything down, diet is critical and having the right foods and beverages on hand is very important. You'll want to pick up lots of fruits and vegetables, whether they are your favorites or not. This is about replacing the toxins that are leaving your body with good things that are going to make you feel better, and Cheetos or Moon Pies aren't going to cut it. Berries are an excellent snack that contain natural sugar, which is something that ex-drinkers tend to crave. Oats are also good for controlling blood sugar and serve as a relaxant. Bananas are great for lifting mood and a great source of energy, fiber and potassium. Also pick up some food that is high in protein, like chicken, fish or even peanut butter. When you do eat, it's ok to only eat in small portions. Don't force yourself to eat large meals as this isn't necessary.

Finally, the intake of fluids cannot be stressed enough. It's crucial that you drink moderate to large amounts of water. Do not consume more than 2 quarts in an hour, however. It is ok to mix in a few sports drinks for flavor but try to stick primarily to water for fluid intake. Staying hydrated will help the withdrawal symptoms be less severe and allow the alcohol to flush out of your system more quickly. Stay away from caffeinated drinks like coffee and tea. Your sleep patterns will already be very disturbed. These drinks will only exacerbate that and will not help to keep you hydrated.

## Other Activities

Other things you'll want to do during detox to ease symptoms include taking frequent baths, or sitting in a pool if you have one available. The water temperature should really be to your comfort - whatever is going to make you feel better and more comfortable at that moment. It could be the complete opposite just a little while later. Mild exercise, such as stretching and going for a short walk, may also help with circulation and anxiety through the release of endorphins. Rest when you are able and keep your mind busy when you aren't. Don't worry about what time it is or isn't. Your body clock isn't going to be right for quite some time so sleep when you can. When you can't sleep, keep your mind occupied with those books or movies that you have on hand and planning that wonderful new life free from alcohol that you have in front of you.

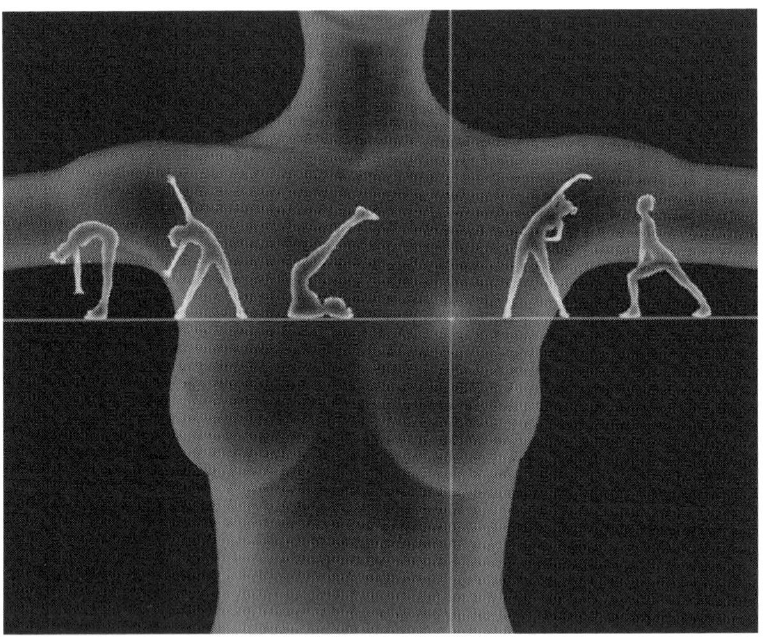

## After Alcohol Detox

*Life is not always what one wants it to be, but to make the best of it as it is, is the only way of being happy. -Jennie Jerome Churchill*

After about 36 hours, you will be generally uncomfortable and mostly irritable for the rest of the week. Continue with your detox routine, healthy diet, vitamins, supplements, moderate exercise and intermittent sleep. In less than a week, you should be ready to resume some "normal" activities provided they are not too stressful. What's most important to note here is that you've simply detoxed from alcohol, nothing else. You have successfully gotten the toxins out of your system but, unless you make some other changes in your life, you will more than likely end up right back where you were a week ago - or worse. To prevent this from happening requires several things:

Coming to the understanding that Alcoholism (and Addiction) is a Disease - read the Disease Chapter.
Considering getting additional help or treatment
Finding a good support network

Otherwise, you have successfully detoxed from alcohol at home. It likely wasn't fun and not something that you would want to repeat or even do over and over again. If that's the case, please check out those final chapters in the book and the Resource Section before moving on.

# Opiate Detox at Home

*When we are no longer able to change a situation - we are challenged to change ourselves. Viktor E. Frankl*

Opiates can be found in both illegal and prescription drugs and are considered to be some of the most addicting substances that people struggle with. Whether it be Heroin, Hydrocodone (Vicodin, Lortab, Percocet), or Oxycodone, they are all highly addictive and the detox from them is quite unpleasant. These drugs serve to mimic the natural painkilling neurotransmitters in the brain, which is what creates the high. However, in long term use of opiates, the brain produces less of these substances, causing detox from opiates to be quite painful. While highly unpleasant, opiate withdrawal is not considered to be life threatening. This does not mean that you wouldn't benefit from a controlled, medically supervised environment. On the contrary, a formal detox facility would make your experience much more comfortable. However, as we discussed at the beginning of the book, there are a lot of valid reasons for wanting to do this at home and this is certainly possible with opiates.

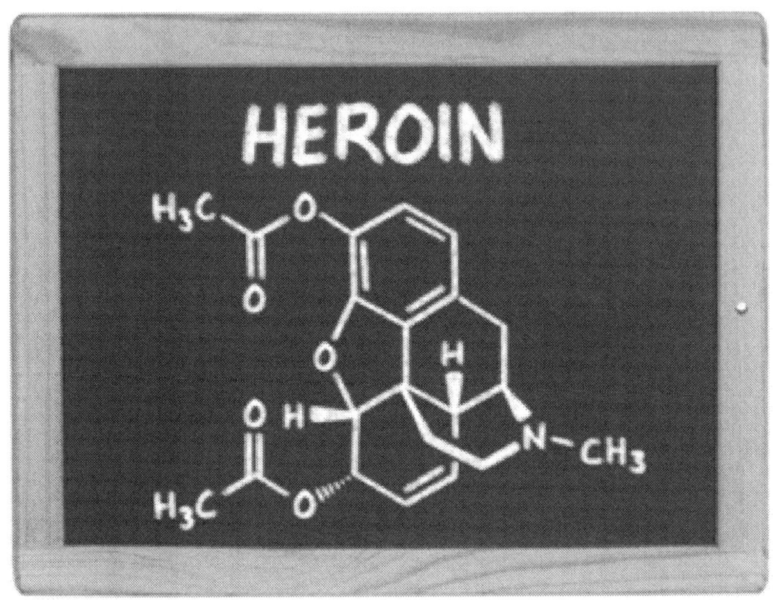
HEROIN
H3C
O
O
O
H
O
H
N
CH3
H3C
O
O

## Special Considerations in Detoxing from Opiates

One thing that you will need to consider before detoxing from opiates is, why you were taking them in first place. If you were taking pain killers for a legitimate pain issue that still needs to be managed, this will need to be addressed. There are some non-opiate treatments for pain that exist and you will need to consult with a specialist, being brutally honest, in order to get the help that you need.

Another consideration with opiates is the possibility of tapering. Some are able to do this successfully and then quit "cold turkey" from a much lower level opiates, lessening the withdrawal symptoms. If you do decide to try tapering with opiates, check out the hard rules for tapering listed in the first section of the book and be sure to stick to them. Regardless, you will still need to prepare for the eventual withdrawal symptoms.

## About Maintenance Drugs: Suboxone, Buprenorphine and Methadone

Methadone has been around for many many years as a legal maintenance drug for opiate addicts, but the last 15 years or so have seen the addition of two new, very powerful, medications called Buprenorphine and Suboxone. Don't be fooled - these are all opiates and highly addictive. The difference is that they have incredibly long half lifes. What this means is that you are not necessarily "getting high" from these medications but you are being affected and the effects are stacking up day after day as yesterdays dose has yet to fully metabolize before you are getting today's dose - and so on. In fact, the newest drug Suboxone is considered to be 25-45 times as potent as morphine. European countries have been using these drugs much longer than in the United States and, in Scandinavia, Buprenorphine is the country's most abused drug. Buprenorphine is now the 41st most prescribed drug in the U.S. These drugs can be used for detoxing from opiates, however, it needs to be done under close medical supervision and consider very carefully any suggestion that they be used for long-term maintenance. You will more than likely just be trading one problem for another and have to go through another detox (covered later) at some later date. Detox from these long-acting opiates is much more severe and can last months. I know this from personal experience.

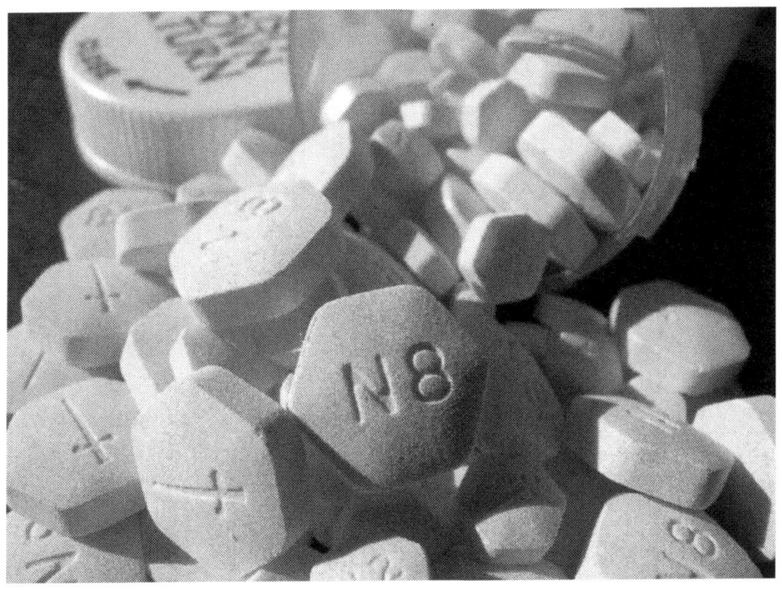
N8

## What to Expect When You Detox From Opiates at Home

Opiate withdrawal actually shares many symptoms with a (very) bad case of the flu. Expect that you will lose your appetite, feel like sleeping or just be run down and suffer from general feelings of illness. Onset of symptoms will depend upon the drug that you are detoxing from. The shorter the half life of the drug, the quicker will be the onset of withdrawal. For example, heroin withdrawal will begin from 8-12 hours after the last dose, with symptoms lasting 5-7 days. The "acute phase" of detox from opiates can last up to 14 days, with the worst part being over in less than 5 days, depending on the drugs and amounts taken. Opiate withdrawal symptoms are characterized by:

- watery eyes
- runny nose
- anxiety
- insomnia
- dilated pupils
- gooseflesh
- muscle aches and joint pain
- abdominal cramps
- nausea and vomiting
- diarrhea
- hot and cold flashes

The post-acute withdrawal symptoms (PAWS) of insomnia, fatigue and mild anxiety can last for many months after stopping taking the drugs. This is the period of time in which the body's opiate receptors heal and the body learns to produce its own endorphins again. You can help this along through moderate exercise and good nutrition, as well as seeking out some sort of a support network (see final chapters of book on this).

# Preparation for Detoxing From Opiates at Home

*Self-discipline is self-caring. -M. Scott Peck*

If you are planning to detox from any sort of opiates at home, be sure to review the general home detox guide in the first chapter that applies to all home detox procedures. Aside from that, you'll need to make some special preparations with respect to detoxing from opiates at home.

## Prepare the Environment

Again, one of the reasons that you are likely choosing to do this at home instead of in an institution is "comfort". If so, be sure that you have everything on hand to make your stay as comfortable, and safe, as possible. Detoxing from opiates and their withdrawal doesn't last as long as some others but don't expect to be hitting the mall or the beach while it's happening. You will be home for the duration so have something to keep yourself busy, whether it be books, movies, games, etc. Also, get rid of all of the drugs in the home. This should be a no brainer but it needs to be said. This is no joke. There is no "saving some for an emergency". If you've gone through the exercise in which you address "Why you are doing this", there shouldn't be much resistance here. Just get rid of them - toss them or give them away immediately. Trust me - you will not be able to resist the temptation once the withdrawal symptoms set in.

**Support**

Did you line up a family member or friend to come and stay with you? If not, do so now. This needs to happen from Day 1, as opiate detox can by psychologically very difficult. Probably after Day 3 or 4, you will be in the clear and they can just check on you, but this will vary on a case by case basis.

Also, try to get an appointment with your family physician and request a prescription for a long-acting benzo such as Valium or Librium. Let your physician know what you are trying to do and that you simply want to take a reducing dose of this medication over the course of several days to lessen the withdrawal symptoms. Your doctor will help with proper dosage. However, if you already have Valium or Librium on hand (don't use other Benzos - they're not the same), this is simply an approximation (using Valium) or example for your reference only:

Day 1: 10mg 4 times a day
Day 2: 10 mg 4 times a day
Day 3: 5 mg 4 times a day
Day 4: 5 mg 4 times a day
Day 5: 5 mg 4 times a day
Day 6: 5 mg morning

If you are unable to get prescription medication to ease the symptoms, you can still find some comfort with over-the-counter medicines, supplements, vitamins and diet.

Here are some over-the-counter medications that you'll want to pick up and their uses:

- **Imodium (Loperamide)** - This is a must-have. It can help with the diarrhea that is likely to come and the gastrointestinal symptoms. Also, it is structurally similar to Demerol and can ease the overall harshness of the detox.

- **Benadryl (Diphenhydramine)** - This is another highly recommended. This can help with anxiety, restlessness, insomnia and the cold-like symptoms. Take 25-50 mgs every 6 hours as needed.
- **Topical Creams containing Methyl Salicylate (Bengay, Icy Hot)** - for joint and muscle pain.
- **Calcium Carbonate (Tums)** - 1 to 2 tablets every 8 hours for abdominal pain and indigestion.
- **OTC Pain Reliever** such as Tylenol, Aleve, Aspirin or Ibuprofen.

As for vitamins and supplements, here are the things that you'll want to consider picking up if your budget allows (you had money for your drugs, didn't you?). Simply stick with the recommended dosages for all of these:

- Vitamin B6 caps
- Vitamin C
- Vitamin E
- Calcium
- Magnesium
- L-Glutamine
- Melatonin
- Valerian Root
- Passion Flower
- Milk Thistle

**If you can find the 1st five of these in a good multi-vitamin, that's fine too.

**Diet**

When we don't feel well, or are anticipating not feeling well, it's tempting to grab a bunch of "comfort foods" and sustain ourselves on them. In this case, that would be a mistake. Chips and cookies are not going to give our liver the nutrients that it needs as it is over-working to detoxify our body from these mass amounts of opiates that have built up in it. You'll want to reduce the load on your liver by minimizing the processed foods and saturated fats that you put in your body. If you're not feeling well, it's ok to eat in small amounts but when you do eat something, eat the right things and stock up on some of this stuff:

- Fiber-rich fruits and vegetables
- Healthy proteins from chicken, fish and eggs
- Plant proteins such as beans and peas
- Healthy fats from fish
- Nuts, seeds, extra virgin olive oil

Also, fluid intake is critical. Drink lots of water. Stay away from soda and coffee for at least 3 weeks. Your sleep patterns will already be disturbed and these are not going to help. Green tea is also ok to drink and is good for its antioxidants and anti inflammatory properties. It's ok to have a few sports drinks for flavor but stick mostly to good old fashioned water - and lots of it.

**Other Activities**

When the detox and withdrawal process starts, there is nothing else to do but ride it out and take it day by day or, if necessary, hour by hour. Don't forget to sleep when you are able, which for some people may be all the time, and to simply keep yourself occupied when you aren't. If you are prepared, you have some movies, books or something else to keep yourself busy for next several days during the periods that you are unable to sleep. Use hot and cool baths to get comfortable as needed and as often as you like. If you have access to a swimming pool or hot tub and it helps, don't think twice about sitting in there all day long if you need to. Also, consider that a small amount exercise can go a long way in making you feel better. Those cramped muscles can be stretched and some endorphins can be released, which is so very important to your well-being. This can be as simple as a 5-10 minute walk. Finally, don't be too hard on yourself and don't forget why you are doing this. Hopefully you went through some sort of exercise in self examination before beginning this process so that you know why it is that you are giving up these drugs and what positive things you hope to gain from a life without them.

# After Opiate Detox

*"...the greater part of our happiness or misery depends on our dispositions and not on our circumstances." -Martha Washington*

The acute phase of opiate withdrawal can be over in as little as 3 days. That's just it though, the withdrawal phase and the toxins leaving your body. It certainly wasn't fun but all of that suffering would be for nothing if you were to walk right back out into the "real world" and resume use. This is an ongoing issue with opiate addiction and the list of things that opiate addicts simply do not understand include:

Addiction is a bona fide disease (Read the Disease Chapter - this is important)
Additional help or treatment is available and probably recommended
Finding a good support network is critical to remaining clean long term

Otherwise, you have successfully detoxed from opiates at home. Maybe this wasn't the first time. Regardless, it likely wasn't fun and not something that you would want to repeat or even do over and over again. If that's the case, please check out those final chapters in the book and the Resource Section before moving on.

# Cocaine Detox at Home

*It is during our darkest moments that we must focus to see the light. -Aristotle Onassis*

Whether smoked, injected or snorted, cocaine works in the brain to create a massive increase in the pleasure and euphoria producing neurotransmitter dopamine. Cocaine users feel energized while high and have a boost of confidence and euphoria, followed by feelings of depression and anxiety when the brain suffers a rebound and the high disappears. Seemingly, the only way forward is to get more cocaine and this sets up the intense cravings that the drug is known for. It's an endless cycle and one that many are looking to break once and for all.

There are many drugs that should, in theory, have some sort of a "medical detox" because of the physical dependency and severity of withdrawal symptoms. Examples are alcohol, opiates, and benzodiazepines. Cocaine is considered to be primarily a "mental addiction". However, the withdrawal symptoms are very real and do have some very real physical components to them. Detoxing from cocaine should not be taken lightly by any means and the mental component to the withdrawal can be absolutely overwhelming for many people, particularly if they have some other mental instabilities already existing.

## Special Considerations in Detoxing from Cocaine

When you decide to detox from cocaine at home, take into consideration a few things. One is your overall physical and mental health otherwise. Now, it's understandable that most drug addicts are not the picture of mental and physical health. That's not what we're talking about here. Do you have any overriding medical issues that could cause complications or any mental disorders that need to be managed in a professional setting? If so, you may wish to consider a private detox facility for a few days just to be monitored.

One thing to consider is that cocaine can cause a lot of damage to the heart. The chronic use of cocaine can damage the heart and lead to an increased likelihood of heart attack, stroke, or death from other cardiopulmonary conditions. Cocaine can cause heart damage in a number of ways, such as:

- Cocaine causes blood pressure to rise after ingestion – which can lead to stroke or ruptured blood vessels in the brain
- Cocaine causes a thickening of the blood vessels which results in diminished supply of oxygen to the brain and muscles. Cocaine also causes the heart to beat more quickly, which compounds the stress and can lead to heart attack or stroke
- A cocaine overdose can lead to sudden heart failure
- Cocaine can lead to an inflammation of the heart muscle (myocarditis) or of the heart lining (Endocarditis)
- Cocaine can cause fluid to gather in the lungs (Pulmonary edema)
- Cocaine can lead to clots in blood vessels (thrombosis)
- The chronic use of cocaine can lead to an enlarged and weakened heart (dilated cardiomyopathy).

So, if you have, or suspect you have, any heart-related issues, please consider a monitored detox. Otherwise, cocaine detox at home with the right preparations is manageable.

## What to Expect When You Detox From Cocaine at Home

Although cocaine produces no physical withdrawal symptoms like vomiting or shaking, it is considered to be an extremely difficult drug to detox from due to the extreme nature of the cravings, agitation and irritability that occur during the withdrawal phase. The first stage of withdrawal can start within 12 hours and last from 4-7 days.

First Stage Symptoms include:

- Irritability
- Severe depression
- Nervousness and anxiety
- Paranoia
- excessive sleepiness, low energy
- excessive appetite
- aching muscles
- possible abdominal pain
- possible chills

Second Stage of withdrawal starts at 7-10 days and gradually decreases over 6 weeks. These symptoms can last for several months, however, and include:

- Depression
- Low energy
- Anhedonia - difficulty experiencing pleasure
- Drug "cravings"

If some of these sound scary, you're right. They are. They psychological effect of taking away this addictive substance is acute and something that you need to be prepared for. Detox from cocaine needs to be focused primarily on managing cravings and mood more than anything else. If you can get through the initial phase of withdrawals and cravings, with solid reminders of why you are doing this and what sorts of benefits you stand gain, you have a much greater chance of success. There are still other preparations that you can make beforehand to make your detox much more comfortable.

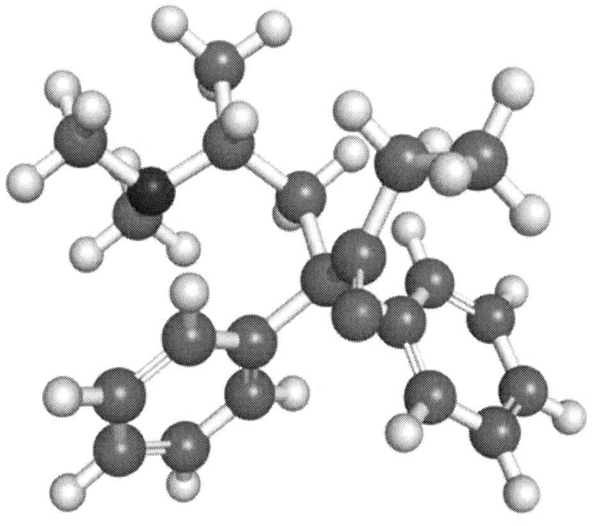

## Preparation for Detoxing From Cocaine at Home

*If there is no struggle, there is no progress. -Frederick Douglass*

If you are planning to detox from cocaine at home, be sure to review the general home detox guide in the first chapter that applies to all home detox procedures. Aside from that, you'll need to make some special preparations with respect to detoxing from cocaine at home.

### Prepare the Environment

Again, one of the reasons that you are likely choosing to do this at home instead of in a detox facility or hospital is "comfort". If so, be sure that you have everything on hand to make your stay as comfortable, and safe, as possible. Detoxing from cocaine and its withdrawal doesn't last as long as some others but don't expect to be heading out to work or taking care of the kids while it's happening. You will be home for the duration so have something to keep yourself busy, whether it be books, movies, games, etc. Also, get rid of all of the drugs in the home. This should be a no brainer but it needs to be said. This is no joke. There is no "saving some for a rainy day". If you've gone through the exercise in which you address "Why you are doing this", there shouldn't be much resistance here. Just get rid of it - toss it or give it away immediately. Trust me - you will not be able to resist the temptation once the withdrawal symptoms set in. Your success or failure could hinge on this single step.

**Support**

Did you line up a family member or friend to come and stay with you? If not, do so now. This needs to happen from Day 1, as cocaine detox can by psychologically very difficult. Probably after Day 3 or 4, you will be in the clear and they can just check on you, but this will vary on a case by case basis.

There really are not any prescription medications that are specifically recommended to help with cocaine detox. If you have an incredibly understanding physician you may wish to ask for a small quantity of long-acting benzos (such as Valium) to take over the course of 5-6 days to help with the anxiety (see opiate detox for dosages). Otherwise, this isn't necessary and there are not any other recommended prescriptions for a home detox. Regardless, you can still find some comfort with over-the-counter medicines, supplements, vitamins and diet.

Here are some over-the-counter medications that you'll want to pick up and their uses:

- **Benadryl (Diphenhydramine)** - This one is highly recommended. This can help with anxiety, restlessness, insomnia and the cold-like symptoms. Take 25-50 mgs every 6 hours as needed.
- **Topical Creams containing Methyl Salicylate (Bengay, Icy Hot)** - for any joint and muscle pain.
- **Calcium Carbonate (Tums)** - 1 to 2 tablets every 8 hours for abdominal pain and indigestion.

As for vitamins and supplements, here are the things that you'll want to consider picking up if your budget allows (you had money for your drugs, didn't you?). Simply stick with the recommended dosages for all of these:

- Vitamin B
- Vitamin C

- Vitamin E
- Calcium
- Magnesium
- Thiamin
- Niacin
- L-Glutamine
- Milk Thistle (helps with liver repair)
- Valerian Root
- Passion Flower

**If you can find the 1st five of these in a good multi-vitamin, that's fine too.

**Diet**

When we don't feel well, or are anticipating not feeling well, we may be inclined to grab a bunch of "comfort foods" and sustain ourselves on them. In this case, that would be a mistake. Chips and cookies are not going to give our heart and liver the nutrients that they need as they are over-working to detoxify our body from these mass amounts of toxins that have built up in it. You'll want to reduce the load on your liver by minimizing the processed foods and saturated fats that you put in your body. With cocaine detox, generally your appetite will increase. This is great because chances are you've been starving yourself and are undernourished right now. However, make the right choice and put some good things in your body for once. On the flip side, if you're not feeling well, it's ok to eat in small amounts but when you do eat something, eat the right things. Either way, stock up on some of this stuff:

- Fiber-rich fruits and vegetables
- Healthy proteins from chicken, fish and eggs
- Plant proteins such as beans and peas
- Healthy fats from fish
- Nuts, seeds, extra virgin olive oil

Also, fluid intake is very important during detox and withdrawal. Drink a ton of water. Stay away from soda and coffee for at least a few weeks if you can. This isn't as crucial as with some of the other detoxes as you will sleep a lot with cocaine detox. So, if you would like an occasional cup of coffee, that's probably ok but keep it to that. Green tea is also ok to drink and is good for its antioxidants and anti inflammatory properties. It's ok to have a few sports drinks for flavor but stick mostly to good old fashioned water - and lots of it.

**Other Activities**

It's ok to sleep as much as you want and when you feel your body needs it during this process. However, detox and withdrawal from cocaine is a highly mental process and it's important to manage this above all else. Have a support person there with you and have things available to keep you occupied and distracted. Inspirational books and movies would be great for this process if you are going to stay at home. If you are going to go out, the recommendation would be that you find a 12 Step meeting and get some further support there. It's imperative that you stay away from other stimulants, including alcohol and other drugs, during this process. They will only serve to lead you back to your drug of choice. It's also important that you stay away from people who use drugs or any other "triggers" that may make this process even more difficult for you. Triggers can be people, places or things that remind you of using or that could initiate those drug cravings. Finally, consider that a small amount of exercise can go a long way in making you feel better. Just a 10 minute walk can release some of those endorphins that are no longer being released by the drugs and give you a sense of well-being. Do this each day and you will be amazed with the results.

## After Cocaine Detox

*If we don't change, we don't grow. If we don't grow, we aren't really living. -Gail Sheehy*

The acute phase of cocaine withdrawal can be over in as little as 4 days. That's just it though, the withdrawal phase and the residual toxins leaving your body. It certainly wasn't fun but all of that suffering would be for nothing if you were to walk right back out into the "real world" and resume use. Cravings can continue to be intense and a cocaine habit is incredibly hard to break, almost impossible to do alone. This is why digesting the following information is so important:

Addiction is a bona fide disease (Read the Disease Chapter - this is important)
Additional help or treatment is available and probably recommended
Finding a good support network is critical to remaining clean long term

Otherwise, you have successfully detoxed from cocaine at home. Maybe this wasn't the first time. Regardless, it more than likely wasn't fun and not something that you would want to repeat or even do over and over again. If that's the case, please check out those final chapters in the book and the Resource Section before moving on.

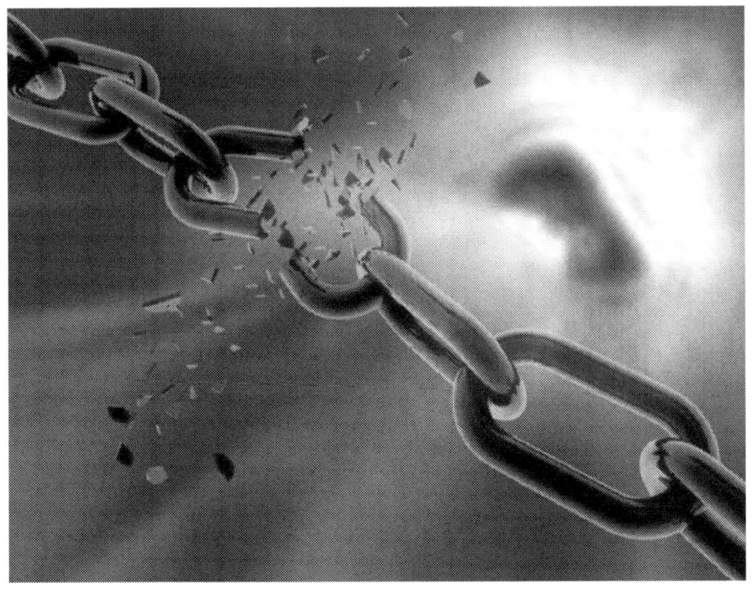

# Benzo Detox at Home

*Believe you can and you're halfway there. -Theodore Roosevelt*

Benzodiazepines, or Benzos, are medications that are prescribed generally to treat anxiety and panic disorders. Some of the commonly prescribed drugs are Klonopin, Xanax, Librium, Restoril, Rohypnol and Valium. Use of benzos, either therapeutically or recreationally, can lead to insomnia, amnesia, hostility, irritability and disturbing dreams. Benzos target the limbic system of the brain as opposed to the entire central nervous system. This means that use of them may lead to fewer long-term effects, yet they are still only meant to be taken for a short period of treatment.

When used repeatedly over a long period of time, tolerance for the pills will develop, requiring users to increase their dosage in order to obtain the desired effects. Also, over an extended period of time, users almost always find themselves unable to sleep without the aid of them. In fact, many develop a recurrence and increase in the symptoms that prompted them to start taking the medication in the first place - such as anxiety, depression and irritability. So, obviously the long-term benefits of coming off of Benzos would be decreased depression and anxiety, improved physical and mental health, and potentially a reduced risk of suicide. What many who begin taking Benzos in the first place aren't told is that they are highly addictive and very dangerous to detox from. In fact, a great deal of care and planning needs to take place if this is something that you are determined to do on your own. Even then, you must still enlist some help.

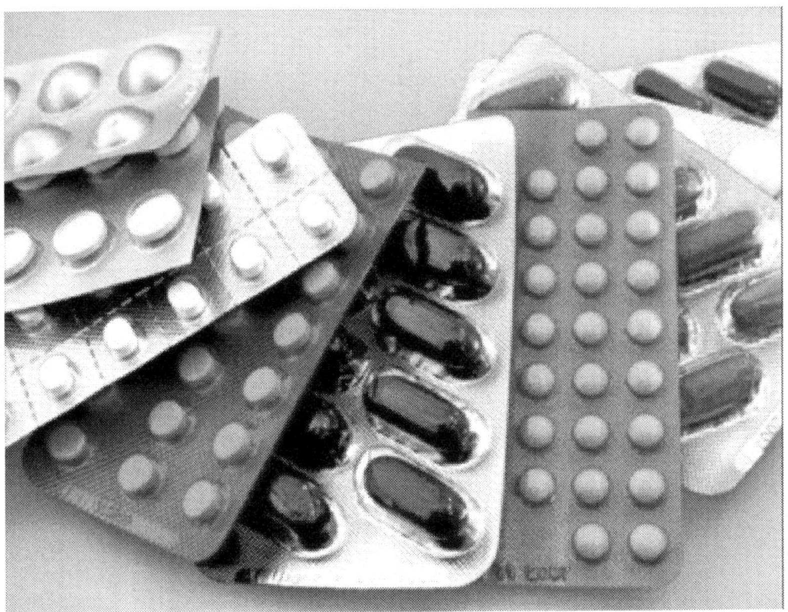

## Benzodiazepine Detox and the Importance of Tapering

You cannot just stop takings Benzos "cold turkey". It is entirely too dangerous and can result in severe withdrawal symptoms such as seizures, psychosis and suicide. There are some detox facilities that will do a "cold turkey" detox with the help of a 7 day course of phenobarbitol to ease the symptoms. This is also not recommended because, once that course is completed and the phenobarbitol wears off, the onset of delayed and severe Benzo withdrawals will often kick in and you will be just as miserable as ever. Other detox facilities may use what is called a "flumazenil detox". This is supposed to wipe out your tolerance that has been built up and prevent withdrawal symptoms when the benzos are removed. There is debate on this one because of inconsistent results - ie - it works great for some and causes others to have suicidal ideation. Again, if you choose to try something like this, be sure to do your homework. Otherwise, tapering is highly recommended when you detox from Benzos.

Tapering refers to slowly reducing the amount of the drug that you are taking over a period of time in order to lessen, or eliminate, withdrawal symptoms. With respect to Benzos, this is the recommended, and safest, course of action. The tough part comes in creating a specific plan for your detox and tapering based on your circumstances. An important thing to remember when putting your plan together for Benzo Detox is that it's better to reduce too slowly than to reduce too quickly. Several things to consider are: what drug(s) you are taking, quantity taken per day and length of time you have been taking the drugs. The third item is not as important as the first two but consider that someone that has been dependent upon Xanax for 3 months may have an easier time with detox than someone that has been taking it for 10 years.

Once you have this information together, consider that you are going to be much more comfortable if you can "cross over" your current benzodiazepine use to the equivalent dose of Diazepam (aka - Valium). If your Benzo "of choice" is already Valium, no switching is needed.

Here is the reason: **drug half life**. Many Benzos, like Xanax, are short acting and result in the rising and falling of the quantities of the medication in your bloodstream many times over the course of a day, which can lead to feelings of withdrawal and cravings. Longer acting medications, like Valium, result in more stable blood concentrations. Valium has a half life of up to 200 hours, meaning that the blood level for each dose falls by half in about 8.3 days. There are a few other similar Benzos but Valium (Diazepam) is also recommended because you can obtain it in 2mg tablets, which can also be halved to 1mg tabs if necessary.

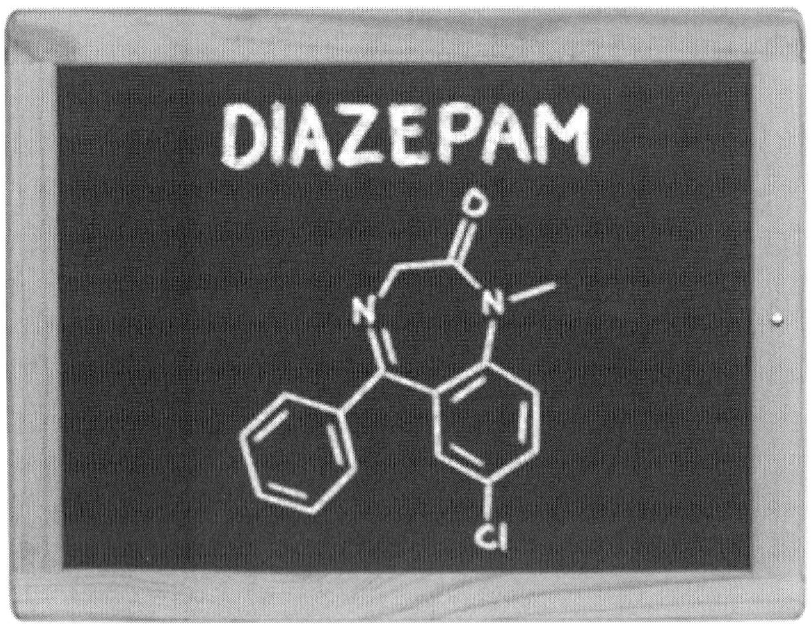


First let's take a look at the approximate equivalent dosages of Diazepam (Valium) for other Benzos that you may be taking:

The approximate equivalent dose to 10mg diazepam (Valium) are given below:

| Benzodiazepines | Half-Life (hrs), [active metabolite] | Approximate Equivalent Oral Dosages (mg) |
|---|---|---|
| Alprazolam (Xanax) | 6-12 | 0.5 |
| Chlordiazepam (Librium) | 5-30 [36-200] | 5-6 |
| Clonazepam(Klonopin, Rivotril) | 18-50 | 0.5 |
| Flunitrazepam (Rohypnol) | 18-26 [36-200] | 10 |
| Lorazepam (Ativan) | 10-20 | 1 |
| Oxazepam (Serax, Serenid D) | 4-15 | 20 |
| Temazepam (Restoril) | 8-22 | 20 |
| Triazolam (Halcion) | 2 | 0.5 |

For example, if you were taking 1mg of Ativan per day, this would be the equivalent of 10mg of Valium. 2mg of Halcion per day would be the equivalent of 40mg of Valium and 100mg of Restoril per day would be the equivalent of 50mg of Valium.

Now that we have that figured out, is it as simple as just switching out one for the other and then tapering off? No, not even close. Unfortunately, the "cross over" needs to be done in a gradual or step-wise fashion or there could be dire consequences. One reason for this is, though we gave you a fancy looking equivalency chart (above), these are not precise and the way that these metabolize in your body could be slightly different. Also, Valium may have a slightly different profile of action than the Benzo that you are used to taking, ie - perhaps less hypnotic activity. This may result in more or less sleepiness and a change in anxiety levels. This is why substitutions of Valium are done gradually over time and not all at once. Then, once you are exclusively on an equivalent dose of Valium, further tapering can begin. Again, the longer the better and the more time and thought that you put into your detox plan, the greater your chances for success and the better you'll be able to manage Benzo withdrawals, or avoid them altogether.

Here are some tapering examples used by actual patients that have detoxed from specific Benzos. These outline the schedule by which you would "cross over" gradually to the equivalent dose of Valium and the tapering schedule based on the Benzo being detoxed from. When viewing these schedules, remember that these are examples only and that every individual is different - has a different body chemistry, was likely on these drugs a different period of time than you were and may have, or not have, other physical and/or mental conditions that affected the outcome of this. In other words, this is absolutely not medical advice and you would be wise to consult your physician before moving forward. Benzo Tapering Examples:

**Table 1** - Withdrawal from Lorazepam (Ativan) 6mg/day:

| **Withdrawal from lorazepam (Ativan) 6mg daily with diazepam (Valium) substitution. (6mg lorazepam is approximately equivalent to 60mg diazepam)** | | | | |
|---|---|---|---|---|
| | **Morning** | **Midday/ Afternoon** | **Evening /Night** | **Daily Diazepam Equivalent** |
| Starting dosage | lorazepam 2mg | lorazepam 2mg | lorazepam 2mg | 60mg |
| Stage 1 (one week) | lorazepam 2mg | lorazepam 2mg | lorazepam 1mg diazepam 10mg | 60mg |
| Stage 2 (one week) | lorazepam 1.5mg diazepam 5mg | lorazepam 2mg | lorazepam 1mg diazepam 10mg | 60mg |
| Stage 3 (one week) | lorazepam 1.5mg diazepam 5mg | lorazepam 2mg | lorazepam 0.5mg diazepam 15mg | 60mg |
| Stage 4 (one week) | lorazepam 1.5mg diazepam 5mg | lorazepam 1.5mg diazepam 5mg | lorazepam 0.5mg diazepam 15mg | 60mg |
| Stage 5 (1-2 weeks) | lorazepam 1.5mg diazepam 5mg | lorazepam 1.5mg diazepam 5mg | Stop lorazepam diazepam 20mg | 60mg |
| Stage 6 (1-2 weeks) | lorazepam 1mg diazepam 5mg | lorazepam 1.5mg diazepam 5mg | diazepam 20mg | 55mg |
| Stage 7 (1-2 weeks) | lorazepam 1mg diazepam 5mg | lorazepam 1mg diazepam 5mg | diazepam 20mg | 50mg |
| Stage 8 (1-2 weeks) | lorazepam 0.5mg diazepam 5mg | lorazepam 1mg diazepam 5mg | diazepam 20mg | 45mg |
| Stage 9 (1-2 weeks) | lorazepam 0.5mg diazepam 5mg | lorazepam 0.5mg diazepam 5mg | diazepam 20mg | 40mg |
| Stage 10 (1-2 weeks) | Stop lorazepam diazepam 5mg | lorazepam 0.5mg diazepam 5mg | diazepam 20mg | 35mg |
| Stage 11 (1-2 weeks) | diazepam 5mg | Stop lorazepam diazepam 5mg | diazepam 20mg | 30mg |
| Stage 12 (1-2 weeks) | diazepam 5mg | diazepam 5mg | diazepam 18mg | 28mg |
| Stage 13 (1-2 weeks) | diazepam 5mg | diazepam 5mg | diazepam 16mg | 26mg |
| Stage 14 (1-2 weeks) | diazepam 5mg | diazepam 5mg | diazepam 14mg | 24mg |
| Stage 15 (1-2 weeks) | diazepam 5mg | diazepam 5mg | diazepam 12mg | 22mg |
| Stage 16 (1-2 weeks) | diazepam 5mg | diazepam 5mg | diazepam 10mg | 20mg |

| | Morning | Midday/ Afternoon | Evening /Night | Daily Diazepam Equivalent |
|---|---|---|---|---|
| Stage 17 (1-2 weeks) | diazepam 5mg | diazepam 4mg | diazepam 10mg | 19mg |
| Stage 18 (1-2 weeks) | diazepam 4mg | diazepam 4mg | diazepam 10mg | 18mg |
| Stage 19 (1-2 weeks) | diazepam 4mg | diazepam 3mg | diazepam 10mg | 17mg |
| Stage 20 (1-2 weeks) | diazepam 3mg | diazepam 3mg | diazepam 10mg | 16mg |
| Stage 21 (1-2 weeks) | diazepam 3mg | diazepam 2mg | diazepam 10mg | 15mg |
| Stage 22 (1-2 weeks) | diazepam 2mg | diazepam 2mg | diazepam 10mg | 14mg |
| Stage 23 (1-2 weeks) | diazepam 2mg | diazepam 1mg | diazepam 10mg | 13mg |
| Stage 24 (1-2 weeks) | diazepam 1mg | diazepam 1mg | diazepam 10mg | 12mg |
| Stage 25 (1-2 weeks) | diazepam 1mg | Stop diazepam | diazepam 10mg | 11mg |
| Stage 26 (1-2 weeks) | Stop diazepam | -- | diazepam 10mg | 10mg |
| Stage 27 (1-2 weeks) | -- | -- | diazepam 9mg | 9mg |
| Stage 28 (1-2 weeks) | -- | -- | diazepam 8mg | 8mg |
| Stage 29 (1-2 weeks) | -- | -- | diazepam 7mg | 7mg |
| Stage 30 (1-2 weeks) | -- | -- | diazepam 6mg | 6mg |
| Stage 31 (1-2 weeks) | -- | -- | diazepam 5mg | 5mg |
| Stage 32 (1-2 weeks) | -- | -- | diazepam 4mg | 4mg |
| Stage 33 (1-2 weeks) | -- | -- | diazepam 3mg | 3mg |
| Stage 34 (1-2 weeks) | -- | -- | diazepam 2mg | 2mg |
| Stage 35 (1-2 weeks) | -- | -- | diazepam 1mg | 1mg |
| Stage 36 | -- | -- | Stop diazepam | -- |

**Table 2:** Withdrawal from Alprazolam (Xanax) 6mg/day:

| Withdrawal from high dose (6mg) alprazolam (Xanax daily with diazepam (Valium) substitution. (6mg alprazolam is approximately equivalent to 120mg diazepam) | | | | |
|---|---|---|---|---|
| | Morning | Midday/ Afternoon | Evening /Night | Daily Diazepam Equivalent |
| Starting dosage | alprazolam 2mg | alprazolam 2mg | alprazolam 2mg | 120mg |
| Stage 1 (one week) | alprazolam 2mg | alprazolam 2mg | alprazolam 1.5mg diazepam 10mg | 120mg |
| Stage 2 (one week) | alprazolam 2mg | alprazolam 2mg | alprazolam 1mg diazepam 20mg | 120mg |
| Stage 3 (one week) | alprazolam 1.5mg diazepam 10mg | alprazolam 2mg | alprazolam 1mg diazepam 20mg | 120mg |
| Stage 4 (one week) | alprazolam 1mg diazepam 20mg | alprazolam 2mg | alprazolam 1mg diazepam 20mg | 120mg |
| Stage 5 (1-2 weeks) | alprazolam 1mg diazepam 20mg | alprazolam 1mg diazepam 10mg | alprazolam 1mg diazepam 20mg | 110mg |
| Stage 6 (1-2 weeks) | alprazolam 1mg diazepam 20mg | alprazolam 1mg diazepam 10mg | alprazolam 0.5mg diazepam 20mg | 100mg |
| Stage 7 (1-2 weeks) | alprazolam 1mg diazepam 20mg | alprazolam 1mg diazepam 10mg | Stop alprazolam diazepam 20mg | 90mg |
| Stage 8 (1-2 weeks) | alprazolam 0.5mg diazepam 20mg | alprazolam 1mg diazepam 10mg | diazepam 20mg | 80mg |
| Stage 9 (1-2 weeks) | alprazolam 0.5mg diazepam 20mg | alprazolam 0.5mg diazepam 10mg | diazepam 20mg | 80mg |
| Stage 10 (1-2 weeks) | alprazolam 0.5mg diazepam 20mg | Stop alprazolam diazepam 10mg | diazepam 20mg | 60mg |
| Stage 11 (1-2 weeks) | Stop alprazolam diazepam 20mg | diazepam 10mg | diazepam 20mg | 50mg |
| Stage 12 (1-2 weeks) | diazepam 25mg | Stop midday dose; | diazepam 25mg | 50mg |

| | Morning | Midday/ Afternoon | Evening /Night | Daily Diazepam Equivalent |
|---|---|---|---|---|
| Stage 13 (1-2 weeks) | diazepam 20mg | -- | diazepam 25mg | 45mg |
| Stage 14 (1-2 weeks) | diazepam 20mg | -- | diazepam 20mg | 40mg |
| Stage 15 (1-2 weeks) | diazepam 20mg | -- | diazepam 20mg | 40mg |
| Stage 16 (1-2 weeks) | diazepam 18mg | -- | diazepam 20mg | 38mg |
| Stage 17 (1-2 weeks) | diazepam 18mg | -- | diazepam 18mg | 36mg |
| Stage 18 (1-2 weeks) | diazepam 16mg | -- | diazepam 18mg | 34mg |
| Stage 19 (1-2 weeks) | diazepam 16mg | -- | diazepam 16mg | 32mg |
| Stage 20 (1-2 weeks) | diazepam 14mg | -- | diazepam 16mg | 30mg |
| Stage 21 (1-2 weeks) | diazepam 14mg | -- | diazepam 14mg | 28mg |
| Stage 22 (1-2 weeks) | diazepam 12mg | -- | diazepam 14mg | 26mg |
| Stage 23 (1-2 weeks) | diazepam 12mg | -- | diazepam 12mg | 24mg |
| Stage 24 (1-2 weeks) | diazepam 10mg | -- | diazepam 12mg | 22mg |
| Stage 25 (1-2 weeks) | diazepam 10mg | -- | diazepam 10mg | 20mg |
| Stage 26 (1-2 weeks) | diazepam 8mg | -- | diazepam 10mg | 18mg |
| Stage 27 (1-2 weeks) | diazepam 8mg | -- | diazepam 8mg | 16mg |

| | Morning | Midday/ Afternoon | Evening /Night | Daily Diazepam Equivalent |
|---|---|---|---|---|
| Stage 28 (1-2 weeks) | diazepam 6mg | -- | diazepam 8mg | 14mg |
| Stage 29 (1-2 weeks) | diazepam 5mg | -- | diazepam 8mg | 13mg |
| Stage 30 (1-2 weeks) | diazepam 4mg | -- | diazepam 8mg | 12mg |
| Stage 31 (1-2 weeks) | diazepam 3mg | -- | diazepam 8mg | 11mg |
| Stage 32 (1-2 weeks) | diazepam 2mg | -- | diazepam 8mg | 10mg |
| Stage 33 (1-2 weeks) | diazepam 1mg | -- | diazepam 8mg | 9mg |
| Stage 34 (1-2 weeks) | -- | -- | diazepam 8mg | 8mg |
| Stage 35 (1-2 weeks) | -- | -- | diazepam 7mg | 7mg |
| Stage 36 (1-2 weeks) | -- | -- | diazepam 6mg | 6mg |
| Stage 37 (1-2 weeks) | -- | -- | diazepam 5mg | 5mg |
| Stage 38 (1-2 weeks) | -- | -- | diazepam 4mg | 4mg |
| Stage 39 (1-2 weeks) | -- | -- | diazepam 3mg | 3mg |
| Stage 40 (1-2 weeks) | -- | -- | diazepam 2mg | 2mg |
| Stage 41 (1-2 weeks) | -- | -- | diazepam 1mg | 1mg |
| | -- | -- | Stop diazepam | -- |

**Table 3**: Withdrawal from Clonazepam (Klonopin) 1.5mg/day:

**Withdrawal from clonazepam (Klonopin) 1.5mg daily with substitution of diazepam (Valium). (0.5mg clonazepam is approximately equivalent to 10mg diazepam)**

| | Morning | Midday/ Afternoon | Evening /Night | Daily Diazepam Equivalent |
|---|---|---|---|---|
| Starting dosage | clonazepam 0.5mg | clonazepam 0.5mg | clonazepam 0.5mg | 30mg |
| Stage 1 (1 week) | clonazepam 0.5mg | clonazepam 0.5mg | 0.25mg diazepam 5mg | 30mg |
| Stage 2 (1 week) | clonazepam 0.5mg | clonazepam 0.5mg | Stop clonazepam diazepam 10mg | 30mg |
| Stage 3 (1 week) | clonazepam 0.25mg diazepam 5mg | clonazepam 0.5mg | diazepam 10mg | 30mg |
| Stage 4 (1 week) | clonazepam 0.25mg diazepam 5mg | clonazepam 0.25mg diazepam 5mg | diazepam 10mg | 30mg |
| Stage 5 (1 week) | Stop clonazepam diazepam 10mg | clonazepam 0.25mg diazepam 5mg | diazepam 10mg | 30mg |
| Stage 6 (1-2 weeks) | diazepam 10mg | Stop clonazepam diazepam 8mg | diazepam 10mg | 28mg |
| Stage 7 (1-2 weeks) | diazepam 10mg | diazepam 6mg | diazepam 10mg | 26mg |
| Stage 8 (1-2 weeks) | diazepam 10mg | diazepam 4mg | diazepam 10mg | 24mg |
| Stage 9 (1-2 weeks) | diazepam 10mg | diazepam 2mg | diazepam 10mg | 22mg |
| Stage 10 (1-2 weeks) | diazepam 10mg | Stop diazepam | diazepam 10mg | 20mg |
| Stage 11 (1-2 weeks) | diazepam 8mg | -- | diazepam 10mg | 18mg |

| | Morning | Midday/ Afternoon | Evening /Night | Daily Diazepam Equivalent |
|---|---|---|---|---|
| Stage 12 (1-2 weeks) | diazepam 6mg | -- | diazepam 10mg | 16mg |
| Stage 13 (1-2 weeks) | diazepam 4mg | -- | diazepam 10mg | 14mg |
| Stage 14 (1-2 weeks) | diazepam 2mg | -- | diazepam 10mg | 12mg |
| Stage 15 (1-2 weeks) | Stop diazepam | -- | diazepam 10mg | 10mg |
| Stage 16 (1-2 weeks) | -- | -- | diazepam 9mg | 9mg |
| Stage 17 (1-2 weeks) | -- | -- | diazepam 8mg | 8mg |
| Stage 18 (1-2 weeks) | -- | -- | diazepam 7mg | 7mg |
| Stage 19 (1-2 weeks) | -- | -- | diazepam 6mg | 6mg |
| Stage 20 (1-2 weeks) | -- | -- | diazepam 5mg | 5mg |
| Stage 21 (1-2 weeks) | -- | -- | diazepam 4mg | 4mg |
| Stage 22 (1-2 weeks) | -- | -- | diazepam 3mg | 3mg |
| Stage 23 (1-2 weeks) | -- | -- | diazepam 2mg | 2mg |
| Stage 24 (1-2 weeks) | -- | -- | diazepam 1mg | 1mg |
| | -- | -- | Stop diazepam | -- |

**Table 4**: Withdrawal from Temazepam (Restoril) 30mg/day (taken at night):

| **Withdrawal from temazepam (Restoril) 30mg nightly with diazepam substitution. (30mg temazepam is approximately equivalent to 15mg diazepam)** | | |
|---|---|---|
| | **Evening /Night** | **Daily Diazepam Equivalent** |
| Starting dosage | temazepam 30mg | 15mg |
| Stage 1 (1-2 weeks) | temazepam 15mg<br>diazepam 7.5mg | 15mg |
| Stage 2 (1-2 weeks) | temazepam 7.5mg<br>diazepam 12mg | 15.75mg |
| Stage 3 (1-2 weeks) | Stop temazepam<br>diazepam 15mg | 15mg |
| Stage 4 (1-2 weeks) | diazepam 14mg | 14mg |
| Stage 5 (1-2 weeks) | diazepam 13mg | 13mg |
| Stage 6 (1-2 weeks) | diazepam 12mg | 12mg |
| Stage 7 (1-2 weeks) | diazepam 11mg | 11mg |
| Stage 8 (1-2 weeks) | diazepam 10mg | 10mg |
| Stage 9 (1-2 weeks) | diazepam 9mg | 9mg |
| Stage 10 (1-2 weeks) | diazepam 8mg | 8mg |
| Stage 11 (1-2 weeks) | diazepam 7mg | 7mg |
| Stage 12 (1-2 weeks) | diazepam 6mg | 6mg |
| Stage 13 (1-2 weeks) | diazepam 5mg | 5mg |
| Stage 14 (1-2 weeks) | diazepam 4mg | 4mg |
| Stage 15 (1-2 weeks) | diazepam 3mg | 3mg |
| Stage 16 (1-2 weeks) | diazepam 2mg | 2mg |
| Stage 17 (1-2 weeks) | diazepam 1mg | 1mg |
| Stage 18 | Stop diazepam | -- |

## What to Expect When You Detox From Benzodiazepines

If anything has gotten through to you so far, hopefully it is that this is not something to take lightly or jump into without a lot of thought and planning. In fact, you should seriously think about doing this in a medically supervised environment. It would be much safer and your tapering and withdrawal symptoms could be managed by professionals. Even with the "cross over" and tapering, expect that you will experience at least some discomfort and withdrawal symptoms. The onset of withdrawal from Benzos depends on the half-life of the particular drug that you were taking. Once that half-life has elapsed and you haven't taken another pill, symptoms will appear and shorter acting benzodiazepines tend to have more severe withdrawal symptoms. Duration of symptoms can range from 2-4 weeks and may include:

- Anxiety
- Tinnitus
- Tremors
- Insomnia
- Perceptual distortion
- Muscle cramps, muscle twitching
- Paranoia
- Paraesthesia
- Convulsions
- Headache
- Confusion, disorientation
- Nausea, vomiting
- Hallucinations
- Fatigue

Benzos were often prescribed in the first place for anxiety and these feelings have a tendency to return quite quickly once the drugs are removed. This is also why tapering is important. Craving for the drugs can persist for weeks or even months. Benzodiazepines also offer a set of symptoms that are unique to this class of drugs, called Post-Acute Withdrawal Symptoms (PAWS). These persistent symptoms can occur several weeks or months after your last dose of the Benzo and can include: insomnia, depression, anxiety and other mental instabilities. Also, expect that this is going to take some time. If you reviewed those sample schedules, you can see that a long tapering schedule can last anywhere from 6-18 months. Be patient with yourself and you'll be much better off in the long run.

While the road ahead may seem tough, if you have gone through the exercise at the beginning of the book where you take a look at why you are doing this and what you stand to gain, you'll be able to see the light at the end of the tunnel already. There are still other preparations that you can make beforehand to make your detox much more comfortable.

# Preparation for Benzodiazepine Detox at Home

*Find a place inside where there's joy, and the joy will burn out the pain. -Joseph Campbell*

If you are planning to detox from Benzos at home, be sure to review the general home detox guide in the first chapter that applies to all home detox procedures. Aside from that, you'll need to make some special preparations with respect to detoxing from Benzos at home.

## Prepare the Environment

It would be at this point that I would generally tell you to take some time off of work, send the kids away and rent a bunch of movies to pass the time that you will be "holed up" in your home. Not so in this case. In fact, if you are going to need to take some time off and "lay low", it may not be until the very end of the process where you are actually removing the long-acting Valium from your body and may feel crummy and very tired for several days. In general, if you are sticking to a nice slow, long tapering schedule, you should be able to continue with your daily schedule of activities, including work. Don't expect life to be "fun" for awhile, but it should be manageable and safe. That's the point of doing this slowly.

**Support**

Involving your physician in this endeavor is critical. As soon as you commit to detoxing from Benzos and doing this "at home", you need to schedule an appointment with your doctor and let him/her know your plan and request what you need from them. Specifically, you'll want to discuss any other medical or psychological conditions that may interfere with a home detox and also discuss a tapering schedule using Diazepam (Valium). Set a date to start the process and schedule a follow up appointment with your physician sometime in the first 1-2 weeks to follow up and discuss progress.

It would also be a good idea to enlist other people to act as "support" pillars in your detox project. Whether it be family members or close friends, let someone else know what you are doing and why you are doing it. If you think no one knows what has been going on with you, you'd be surprised to find out that the secret has been out for quite some time and that the people that love you really only want the best for you in the end. They'll be supportive and willing to help in any way. You may need help in "doling" out medications so that you aren't tempted to take more than is on your tapering schedule or maybe you just need some encouragement. Either way, get started in setting that up now.

There really are no over the counter meds or other prescriptions that are recommended to help with Benzo detox. There are occasionally prescriptions given to address certain symptoms if they are severe enough and these would need to be managed by your physician. These include Anti-Depressants and Beta Blockers. Otherwise, it's highly cautioned that you not turn to other substances, like alcohol or marijuana, in an effort to ease symptoms as this will just cause more problems later on. However, you will want to increase your vitamin and mineral intake and you can start by picking up some of the following:

- Vitamin B
- Potassium

- Zinc
- Magnesium
- L-Glutamine
- Melatonin
- Valerian Root
- Milk Thistle

**Diet**

When we are anticipating not feeling well, we may be inclined to grab a bunch of "comfort foods" as they are sure to make us feel better and get us through a rough time. In this case, that would be a mistake. Cookies and candy are not going to give our heart and liver the nutrients that they need as they is over-working to detoxify our body from these mass amounts of toxins that have built up in it. You'll want to reduce the load on your liver by minimizing the processed foods and saturated fats that you put in your body. While detoxing from Benzos, generally your appetite will go back and forth. Some days you may not have an appetite at all and others you may be very hungry. If you're not feeling well, it's ok to eat in small amounts but when you do eat something, eat the right things. Either way, stock up on some of this stuff:

- Fiber-rich fruits and vegetables
- Healthy proteins from chicken, fish and eggs
- Plant proteins such as beans and peas
- Healthy fats from fish
- Nuts, seeds, extra virgin olive oil

Also, fluid intake is very important during detox and withdrawal. Drink a ton of water every day. Stay away from excess amounts of soda and coffee for at least a few weeks if you can. This isn't as crucial as with some of the other detoxes as you may be overly tired at times. So, if you would like an occasional cup of coffee, that's probably ok but keep it to that. Green tea is also ok to drink and is good for its antioxidants and anti inflammatory properties. It's ok to have a few sports drinks for flavor but stick mostly to good old fashioned water - and lots of it.

**Other Activities**

It's ok to sleep as much as you want and when you feel your body needs it during this process. However, detox and withdrawal from Benzos is both a physical and a highly mental process and it's important to manage this above all else. Stay in touch with your support people and have them remind of you why you are doing this - we tend to forget when times get tough. Inspirational books and movies would be great for this process if you are going to stay at home for any period of time. If you are going to go out, the recommendation would be that you find a 12 Step meeting and get some further support there. Again, it's imperative that you stay away from other stimulants, including alcohol and other drugs, during this process. They will only serve to lead you back to your drug of choice. Finally, consider that a small amount of exercise can go a long way in making you feel better. Just a 10 minute walk can release some of those endorphins that are no longer being released by the drugs and give you a sense of well-being. Do this each day and you will be amazed with the results.

# After Benzo Detox

*Try to be like the turtle - at ease in your own shell. -Bill Copeland*

The acute phase of Benzodiazepine withdrawal can be over in as little as 7 days after the last pill. That's just it though, the withdrawal phase and the residual toxins leaving your body. Compared to some of the other detox processes, this was a very long one and it would be a shame to screw it up and go back to the endless cycle of Benzodiazepine addiction. The detox certainly wasn't fun but all of that suffering would be for nothing if you were to walk right back out into the "real world" and resume using. Cravings can continue to be intense and a Benzo habit is incredibly hard to break, almost impossible to do alone. This is why digesting the following information is so important:

Addiction is a bona fide disease (Read the Disease Chapter - this is important)
Additional help or treatment is available and probably recommended
Finding a good support network is critical to remaining clean long term

Otherwise, you have successfully detoxed from Benzos at home. Maybe this wasn't the first time. Regardless, it more than likely wasn't fun and not something that you would want to repeat or even do over and over again. If that's the case, please check out those final chapters in the book and the Resource Section before moving on.

# Meth Detox at Home

*Your present circumstances don't determine where you can go; they merely determine where you start. -Nido Qubein*

While Meth is considered an "Amphetamine", it has been given its own chapter due to its widespread use and the unique issues that its abuse and withdrawal symptoms present. Crystal Meth is a stimulant and a highly addictive drug. Also known by the names of "speed", "crystal" and just "meth", the drug is most commonly smoked but is also injected. It is considered to be the most potent form of speed available and works by overwhelming the central nervous system's pleasure receptors. Meth is a mood enhancer and has long-term effects including a loss in pleasure reception in the brain and loss of some bodily functions. The effects of use of this drug include loss of appetite, restlessness, increased respiration, insomnia, mood swings and irritability. Meth can cause problems in the blood vessels and can also lead to respiratory damage. When used in high doses it causes paranoia, agitation, and compulsive behavior.

As with most drugs, when used habitually, a tolerance develops where more of the drug is needed to achieve the desired results. Overdose is also an issue with meth users, resulting in convulsions, seizures and coma. There are many drugs that should, in theory, have some sort of a "medical detox" because of the physical dependency and severity of withdrawal symptoms. Examples are alcohol and benzodiazepines. Meth is considered to be both a physical and mental addiction but the withdrawal from it is not considered to be "life threatening" in most cases. Detoxing from meth should not be taken lightly by any means and the mental component to the withdrawal can be absolutely overwhelming for many people, particularly if they have some other physical impairments or mental instabilities already existing.

If you are considering a detox from meth at home, you should meet some basic criteria.

- Have a safe, comfortable place to go through withdrawal symptoms, away from temptation.
- Not have a history of severe withdrawal symptoms or of trying and failing to withdrawal at home.
- You have no co-occurring medical conditions that would require close observation during this period.
- You have no psychiatric illness and meth-associated psychiatric problems, like psychosis or depression.

## Special Considerations With Meth Addiction

You may have decided that you meet the "criteria" to detox from meth at home. That's great, but before we go any further, consider just a few more things that are particular to meth addiction and the issues that users are left to deal with.

There may be infections, including abscesses (from injection sites) or even skin infections (caused by picking). Lung problems are common from prolonged smoking of the drug, which include painful and difficulty breathing. Meth users also frequently have a lot of dental problems that need to be addressed. These come, in part, from the acidic nature of the drug, lower saliva production of users, cravings for sweet sodas and simply poor dental hygiene over a prolonged period of time. Any or all of these conditions may be ignored during use, yet during and after detox, they can be a significant source of pain and discomfort that can cause issues.

In addition, meth users are also frequently involved in behaviors that place them at risk for a plethora of infections. These include HIV, hepatitis C and other sexually transmitted diseases that should be screened for and treated. Other health issues, such as diabetes or asthma may have gone unchecked and untreated for years and these are also issues that can't be ignored any further.

## What to Expect With Meth Withdrawal

Meth withdrawal is not, by itself, medically dangerous. In general, people coming off of meth need more sleep than normal and will start to feel better after several days. That is not to say that this won't be unpleasant or that there will not be complicating issues. Methamphetamine withdrawal symptoms occur over two phases. The Acute Phase, occurs throughout the first week to 10 days, and common symptoms include:

- Irritability, mood swings
- Intense drug cravings
- Depression
- Anxiety
- Fatigue, other sleep issues
- Agitation
- Paranoia
- Hallucinations
- Inability to concentrate
- Muscles aches and pains

The Protracted Phase of meth withdrawal can last for many weeks or even months after the acute phase and includes such symptoms as:

- Drug cravings
- Problems with memory and clear thinking
- Depression
- Sleeping problems

Why all these symptoms and why do they last so long? Well, several reasons:

1. Chronic meth use depletes the levels of certain neurotransmitters, like dopamine.
2. Chronic meth use causes a reduction of receptors for neurotransmitters, such as dopamine. This means that you have insufficient levels of dopamine and also too few receptors for the little that you have remaining.
3. Chronic meth use causes neurotoxicity (brain damage). This can take a long time to heal and why symptoms such as problems with memory, depression and cravings persist for a prolonged period after you quit.

It is entirely possible, with a meth detox, that the withdrawal symptoms can simply get away from you and be too much to handle in a home setting. In fact, more severe symptoms are likely if you injected drugs, use other drugs alongside meth, are in poor health, or used in high doses at a high frequency. Meth withdrawal becomes dangerous if you begin to experience psychosis and become a danger to yourself or others. There is also danger if you become very depressed and have suicidal thoughts. If any of these occur, and a support person should be around to help "judge", be sure to get yourself to a supervised detox facility or the nearest emergency room for help.

While none of the symptoms of meth withdrawal listed sound like a walk in the park, they are manageable under the right conditions. The psychological effect of taking away a substance that you used on regular, and likely heavy, basis is acute and something that you need to be prepared for. Detox from meth needs to be focused primarily on managing mood and cravings more than anything else. If you can get through the initial phase of withdrawals and cravings, with solid reminders of why you are doing this and what sorts of benefits you stand gain, you have a much greater chance of success. There are still other preparations that you can make beforehand to make your detox much more comfortable.

# Preparation for Methamphetamine Detox at Home

*If you're going through hell, keep going. -Winston Churchill*

If you are planning to detox from meth at home, be sure to review the general home detox guide in the first chapter that applies to all home detox procedures. Aside from that, you'll need to make some special preparations with respect to detoxing from meth at home.

## Prepare the Environment

More than likely, one of the reasons that you are choosing to do this at home instead of in a detox facility or hospital is "comfort". If so, be sure that you have everything on hand to make your stay as comfortable, and safe, as possible. Detoxing from meth and its withdrawal can be a bit of a rollercoaster ride for some so don't expect to be heading out to work or taking care of the kids while it's happening. You will be home for the duration so have something to keep yourself busy, whether it be books, movies, games, etc. Also, get rid of all of the drugs in the home. This should be a no brainer but it needs to be said. This is no joke. There is no "saving some just in case". If you've gone through the exercise in which you address "Why you are doing this", there shouldn't be much resistance here. Just get rid of them - toss them or give them away immediately. Trust me - you will not be able to resist the temptation once the withdrawal symptoms and craving set in. Your success or failure could hinge on this single step.

## Support

Did you line up a family member or friend to come and stay with you? If not, do so now. This needs to happen from Day 1, as meth detox can by psychologically very difficult. Probably after Day 4, you will be in the clear and they can just check on you, but this will vary on a case by case basis.

There really are not any "approved" prescription medications that are specifically recommended to help with meth detox. However, there are some out there that can help in minimizing the more stressful symptoms. If you have an incredibly understanding physician you may wish to ask for the following:

- **Sedative hypnotics** - a small quantity of long-acting benzos (such as Valium) to take over the course of 5-6 days to help with the anxiety (see opiate detox for dosages).
- **Antipsychotics** - Medications like haloperidol or phenothiazine may be used in the first 1-2 weeks to manage any psychosis symptoms.
- **Antidepressants** - These may be prescribed to help ease symptoms usually experienced in early recovery from meth.

Otherwise, these aren't entirely necessary and there are not any other recommended prescriptions for a home detox. Regardless, you can still find some comfort with over-the-counter medicines, supplements, vitamins and diet.

Here are some over-the-counter medications that you'll want to pick up and their uses:

- **Benadryl (Diphenhydramine)** - This is highly recommended. This can help with anxiety, restlessness, and insomnia. Take 25-50 mgs every 6 hours as needed.
- **Topical Creams containing Methyl Salicylate (Bengay, Icy Hot)** - for any joint and muscle pain.

- **Calcium Carbonate (Tums)** - 1 to 2 tablets every 8 hours for abdominal pain and indigestion.
- **OTC Pain Reliever** such as Tylenol, Aleve, Aspirin or Ibuprofen for headaches.

As for vitamins and supplements, here are the things that you'll want to consider picking up if your budget allows (you had money for your drugs, didn't you?). Simply stick with the recommended dosages for all of these:

- Vitamin B
- Vitamin C
- Vitamin E
- Calcium
- Magnesium
- Thiamin
- Niacin
- L-Glutamine
- Milk Thistle (helps with liver repair)
- Valerian Root (very helpful for sleep issues)
- Passion Flower

**If you can find the 1st five of these in a good multi-vitamin, that's fine too.

**Diet**

When we don't feel well, or are anticipating not feeling well, we may be inclined to grab a bunch of "comfort foods" and sustain ourselves on them. In this case, that would be a mistake. Chips and cookies are not going to give our heart and liver the nutrients that they need as they is over-working to detoxify our body from these mass amounts of toxins that have built up in it. You'll want to reduce the load on your liver by minimizing the processed foods and saturated fats that you put in your body. With meth detox, generally your appetite will increase. This is great because chances are you've been starving yourself and are undernourished right now. However, make the right choice and put some good things in your body for once. On the flip side, if you're not feeling well, it's ok to eat in small amounts but when you do eat something, eat the right things. Either way, stock up on some of this stuff:

- Fiber-rich fruits and vegetables
- Healthy proteins from chicken, fish and eggs
- Plant proteins such as beans and peas
- Healthy fats from fish
- Nuts, seeds, extra virgin olive oil

Also, fluid intake is very important during detox and withdrawal. Drink a ton of water. Stay away from soda and coffee for at least a few weeks if you can. This isn't as crucial as with some of the other detoxes as you will sleep a lot with meth detox. So, if you would like an occasional cup of coffee, that's probably ok but keep it to that. Green tea is also ok to drink and is good for its antioxidants and anti inflammatory properties. You may also want to add some cranberry juice to the mix as it helps to purify and cleanse the body. It's ok to have a few sports drinks for flavor but stick mostly to good old fashioned water - and lots of it.

**Other Activities**

It's ok to sleep as much as you want and when you feel your body needs it during this process. However, detox and withdrawal from meth is a highly mental process and it's important to manage this above all else. Have a support person there with you and have things available to keep you occupied and distracted. Inspirational books and movies would be great for this process if you are going to stay at home. If you are going to go out, the recommendation would be that you find a 12 Step meeting and get some further support there. It's imperative that you stay away from other stimulants, including alcohol and other drugs, during this process. They will only serve to lead you back to your drug of choice. It's also important that you stay away from people who use drugs or any other "triggers" that may make this process even more difficult for you. Triggers can be people, places or things that remind you of using or that could initiate those drug cravings. Finally, consider that a small amount of exercise can go a long way in making you feel better. Just a 10 minute walk can release some of those endorphins that are no longer being released by the drugs and give you a sense of well-being. Do this each day and you will be amazed with the results.

## After Meth Detox

*Happiness is not something you postpone for the future; it is something you design for the present.* -*Jim Rohn*

The acute phase of meth withdrawal can be over in as little as 4 days, maybe longer than a week. That's just it though, the withdrawal phase and the residual toxins leaving your body. It certainly wasn't fun but all of that suffering would be for nothing if you were to walk right back out into the "real world" and resume use. Consider that you have won the battle but not "the war". Unless you get some additional help that will teach you how to stay motivated, manage cravings and deal with life without the use of drugs, the road ahead will be very tough. Cravings can continue to be intense and a meth habit is incredibly hard to break, almost impossible to do alone. This is why digesting the following information is so important:

Addiction is a bona fide disease (Read the Disease Chapter - this is important)
Additional help or treatment is available and probably recommended
Finding a good support network is critical to remaining clean long term

Otherwise, you have successfully detoxed from meth at home. Maybe this wasn't the first time. Regardless, it more than likely wasn't fun and not something that you would want to repeat or even do over and over again. If that's the case, please check out those final chapters in the book and the Resource Section before moving on.

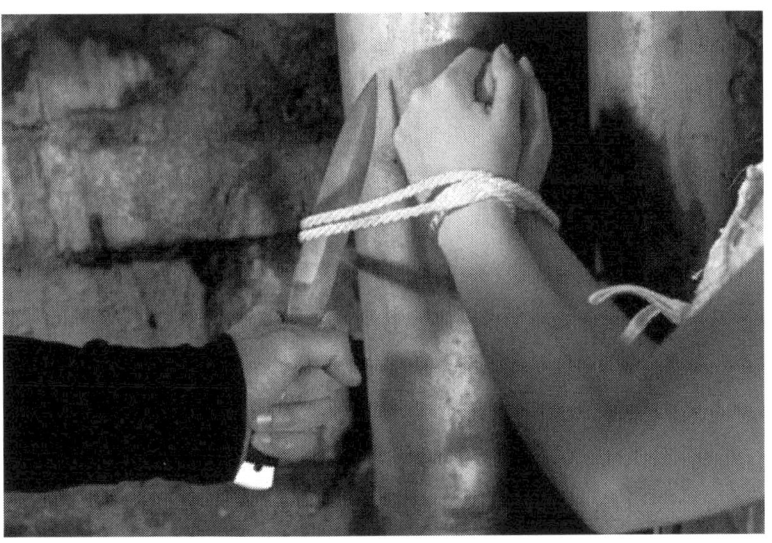

# Amphetamine Withdrawal at Home

*You are never too old to set another goal or to dream a new dream. -C. S. Lewis*

Amphetamine addiction is widespread and this chapter deals with those faced with potential Adderall withdrawal or Ritalin withdrawal and want to handle things from home. Amphetamines are sympathomimetic drugs that act as powerful central nervous system stimulants. They produce many effects, including increased energy, euphoria, increased alertness and decreased appetite. The effects of the drugs have been linked to the actions of numerous neurotransmitters including dopamine, serotonin, norepinephrine and 5-hydroxytryptamine (5-HTP).

The most common forms of Amphetamines are the prescription medications: Adderall, Dexedrine, Dextrostat and Ritalin that are used for the treatment of certain medical conditions including narcolepsy, ADHD and chronic fatigue syndrome. There are also street versions of these drugs in some parts of the world. Whether they be in prescription or "street" form, amphetamines have a very high potential for abuse and have a high risk of addiction. Whether taken in pills, crystals, powders, or liquids, users may ingest, snort, smoke or even inject amphetamines. Once taken, effects can last anywhere from 1-12 hours and tolerance will always develop with heavy, frequent, users.

While there are several drugs that do necessitate you considering a "medical detox", amphetamines are not one of them as detox is not considered to be life threatening, all other things being equal. However, there are some things to consider before you decide to undertake amphetamine withdrawal on your own and at home:

- Have a safe, comfortable place to go through withdrawal symptoms, away from temptation.

- Not have a history of severe withdrawal symptoms or of trying and failing to withdraw at home.
- You have no co-occurring medical conditions that would require close observation during this period.
- You have no psychiatric illness and drug-associated psychiatric problems, like psychosis or depression, are mild.

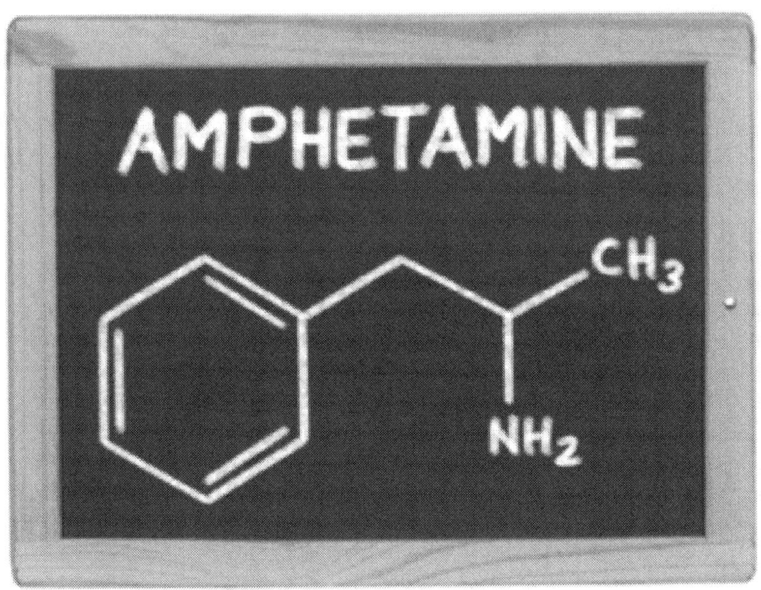

## What to Expect With Amphetamine Withdrawal

Amphetamine withdrawal is not, by itself, medically dangerous. In general, people coming off of Adderall and Ritalin need more sleep than normal and will start to feel better after several days. That is not to say that this won't be unpleasant or that there will not be complicating issues. Amphetamine withdrawal symptoms occur over several phases. A "Crash" Phase will start anywhere from 9-14 hours after the last dose and will last a very short period of time. During this phase you will simply be tired and could sleep around the clock. Other symptoms in this phase could include:

- Anxiety
- Agitation
- Depressive dysphoria

Immediately following this is the Intermediate withdrawal phase, which can last from several days to a week after your last dose of amphetamines, and common symptoms include:

- Fatigue
- Drug cravings
- Changes in sleep patterns
- Paranoia, panic
- Anxiety
- Mood swings
- Depression
- Abdominal pain
- Increased heart rate
- Seizures
- Changes in Appetite

Acute symptoms will peak from 48-72 hours after the last dose, at which time you are at the greatest risk for potential seizures and increased heart rate. Be sure to monitor your condition closely during this period of time and seek immediate medical attention if you feel you need it. There are also long term withdrawal effects from amphetamines to consider. Once the initial phases have passed, withdrawal symptoms can return, many times in the form of intense cravings, for months or even years, often as a result of environmental cues or "triggers".

It is entirely possible, with amphetamine detox, that the withdrawal symptoms can simply get away from you and be too much to handle in a home setting. In fact, more severe symptoms are likely if you injected drugs, use other drugs alongside amphetamines, are in poor health, or used in high doses at a high frequency. Adderall withdrawal and amphetamine withdrawal becomes dangerous if you begin to experience psychosis and become a danger to yourself or others. There is also danger if you become very depressed and have suicidal thoughts. If any of these occur, and a support person should be around to help "judge", be sure to get yourself to a supervised detox facility or the nearest emergency room for help.

While none of the symptoms of amphetamine withdrawal listed above sound like a walk in the park, they are manageable under the right conditions. The psychological effect of taking away a substance that you used on regular, and likely heavy, basis is acute and something that you need to be prepared for. Detox from amphetamines needs to be focused primarily on managing mood and cravings more than anything else. If you can get through the initial phase of withdrawals and cravings, with solid reminders of why you are doing this and what sorts of benefits you stand to gain, you have a much greater chance of success. There are still other preparations that you can make beforehand to make your detox much more comfortable.

## Preparation for Amphetamine Detox at Home

If you are planning to detox from amphetamines at home, be sure to review the general home detox guide in the first chapter that applies to all home detox procedures. Aside from that, you'll need to make some special preparations with respect to amphetamine withdrawal at home.

### Prepare the Environment

More than likely, a few of the reasons that you are choosing to do this at home instead of in a detox facility or hospital are privacy and "comfort". If so, be sure that you have everything on hand to make your stay as comfortable, and safe, as possible. Detoxing from amphetamines and its withdrawal can be a bit of a rollercoaster ride for some so don't expect to be heading out to work or taking care of the kids while it's happening. You will be home for the duration so have something to keep yourself busy, whether it be books, movies, games, etc. Also, get rid of all of the drugs in the home. This should be a no brainer but it needs to be said. This is no joke. There is no "saving some just in case". If you've gone through the exercise in which you address "Why you are doing this", there shouldn't be much resistance here. Just get rid of it - toss it or give it away immediately. Trust me - you will not be able to resist the temptation once the withdrawal symptoms and cravings set in. Your success or failure could hinge on this single step.

## Support

Did you line up a family member or friend to come and stay with you? If not, do so now. This needs to happen from Day 1, as amphetamine detox can be psychologically very difficult. Probably after Day 3 or 4, you will be in the clear and they can just check on you, but this will vary on a case by case basis. Actually, amphetamine detox is one of the "faster" ones to get through because the half life of these drugs are so short. You may be through the worst of it in just a few days time.

There really are not any "approved" prescription medications that are specifically recommended to help with amphetamine detox. However, there are some out there that can help in minimizing the more stressful symptoms. If you have an incredibly understanding physician you may wish to ask for the following:

- **Sedative hypnotics** - a small quantity of long-acting benzos (such as Valium) to take over the course of 5-6 days to help with the anxiety (see opiate detox for dosages).
- **Antipsychotics (Neuroleptics)** - Medications like haloperidol or phenothiazine may be used in the first 1-2 weeks to manage any psychosis symptoms.
- **Antidepressants** - These may be prescribed to help ease symptoms usually experienced in early recovery from amphetamines.

Otherwise, these aren't entirely necessary and there are not any other recommended prescriptions for a home detox. Regardless, you can still find some comfort with over-the-counter medicines, supplements, vitamins and diet.

Here are some over-the-counter medications that you'll want to pick up and their uses:

- **Benadryl (Diphenhydramine)** - This is highly recommended. This can help with anxiety, restlessness, skin sensitivity and insomnia. Take 25-50 mgs every 6 hours as needed.

- **Topical Creams containing Methyl Salicylate (Bengay, Icy Hot)** - for any joint and muscle pain.
- **Calcium Carbonate (Tums)** - 1 to 2 tablets every 8 hours for abdominal pain and indigestion.
- **OTC Pain Reliever** such as Tylenol, Aleve, Aspirin or Ibuprofen for headaches.

As for vitamins and supplements, here are the things that you'll want to consider picking up if your budget allows (you had money for your drugs, didn't you?). Simply stick with the recommended dosages for all of these:

- Vitamin B
- Vitamin C
- Vitamin E
- Calcium
- Magnesium
- Thiamin
- Niacin
- L-Glutamine
- Milk Thistle (helps with liver repair)
- Valerian Root (very helpful for sleep issues)
- Passion Flower

**If you can find the 1st five of these in a good multi-vitamin, that's fine too.

## Diet

When we don't feel well, or are anticipating not feeling well, we may be inclined to grab a bunch of "comfort foods" and sustain ourselves on them. In this case, that would be a mistake. Chips and cookies are not going to give our heart and liver the nutrients that they need as they is over-working to detoxify our body from these mass amounts of toxins that have built up in it. You'll want to reduce the load on your liver by minimizing the processed foods and saturated fats that you put in your body. With amphetamine detox, generally your appetite will increase. This is great because chances are you've been starving yourself and are massively undernourished right now. However, make the right choice and put some good things in your body for once. On the flip side, if you're not feeling well, it's ok to eat in small amounts but when you do eat something, eat the right things. Either way, stock up on some of this stuff:

- Fiber-rich fruits and vegetables
- Healthy proteins from chicken, fish and eggs
- Plant proteins such as beans and peas
- Healthy fats from fish
- Nuts, seeds, extra virgin olive oil

Also, fluid intake is very important during detox and withdrawal. Drink a ton of water. Stay away from soda and coffee for at least a few weeks if you can. This isn't as crucial as with some of the other detoxes as you will sleep a lot with amphetamine detox. So, if you would like an occasional cup of coffee, that's probably ok but keep it to that. Green tea is also ok to drink and is good for its antioxidants and anti inflammatory properties. You may also want to add some cranberry juice to the mix as it helps to purify and cleanse the body. It's ok to have a few sports drinks for flavor but stick mostly to good old fashioned water - and lots of it.

**Other Activities**

It's ok to sleep as much as you want and when you feel your body needs it during this process. However, detox and withdrawal from amphetamines is a highly mental process and it's important to manage this above all else. Have a support person there with you and have things available to keep you occupied and distracted. Inspirational books and movies would be great for this process if you are going to stay at home. If you are going to go out, the recommendation would be that you find a 12 Step meeting and get some further support there. It's imperative that you stay away from other stimulants, including alcohol and other drugs, during this process. They will only serve to lead you back to your drug of choice. It's also important that you stay away from people who use drugs or any other "triggers" that may make this process even more difficult for you. Triggers can be people, places or things that remind you of using or that could initiate those drug cravings. It doesn't matter if you were taking prescription drugs or street drugs, triggers still exist and you need to learn to manage them. Finally, consider that a small amount of exercise can go a long way in making you feel better. Just a 10 minute walk can release some of those endorphins that are no longer being released by the drugs and give you a sense of well-being. Do this each day and you will be amazed with the results.

## After Amphetamine Detox

*After a storm comes a calm.* -*Matthew Henry*

The acute phases of amphetamine withdrawal can be over in as little as 3 days, maybe longer than a week. That's just it though, the withdrawal phase and the residual toxins leaving your body. It certainly wasn't fun but all of that suffering would be for nothing if you were to walk right back out into the "real world" and resume use. Consider that you have won the battle but not "the war". Unless you get some additional help that will teach you how to stay motivated, manage cravings, and deal with life without the use of speed, the road ahead will be very tough. Cravings can continue to be intense and an amphetamine habit is incredibly hard to break, almost impossible to do alone. This is why digesting the following information is so important:

Addiction is a bona fide disease (Read the Disease Chapter - this is important)
Additional help or treatment is available and probably recommended
Finding a good support network is critical to remaining clean long term

Otherwise, you have successfully detoxed from amphetamines at home. Maybe this wasn't the first time. Regardless, it more than likely wasn't fun and not something that you would want to repeat or even do over and over again. If that's the case, please check out those final chapters in the book and the Resource Section before moving on.

# Methadone Detox at Home

*When you reach the end of your rope, tie a knot in it and hang on. -Thomas Jefferson*

Methadone, which also goes by the name Symoron, Dolophine, Amidone, Methadose, Physeptone and Heptadon, is a synthetic opioid that acts upon the same brain receptors that opiates such as hydrocodone and morphine do. Methadone is one of the most physically dependant medications invented in the 20th century. The reasons for this are that it has an extremely long half life (24-36 hours), it is a synthetic morphine, and because of the extreme nature and duration of withdrawal symptoms associated with it. Methadone is often used as both a detox and a maintenance drug for opiate addicts to "recover" without experiencing the full effects of withdrawal when they stop taking their drug of choice, such as Vicodin or Heroin. Unfortunately, Methadone itself is highly addictive, is often abused, and those who use it are required to detox from it when they wish to stop taking it.

All opiates, long-acting or not, serve to mimic the natural painkilling neurotransmitters in the brain. However, in long term use of methadone, the brain produces less of these substances, causing detox from methadone to be quite painful and prolonged. While highly unpleasant, methadone withdrawal is not considered to be life threatening. This does not mean that you wouldn't benefit from a controlled, medically supervised environment. On the contrary, a formal detox facility would make your experience much more comfortable. However, as we discussed at the beginning of the book, there are a lot of valid reasons for wanting to do this at home and this is certainly possible with methadone.

## Special Considerations with Methadone Addiction

One thing that you will need to consider before detoxing from methadone is, why you were taking it in first place. If you were taking the drug for a legitimate pain issue that still needs to be managed, this will need to be addressed. There are some non-opiate treatments for pain that exist and you will need to consult with a specialist, being brutally honest, in order to get the help that you need.

If you have researched methadone detox or opiate detox alternatives, you have likely come across the "Rapid Opiate Detox" method, also known as the Ultra-Rapid Opiate detox, Asturian method, UROD, Detox 5, or Waisssmann Method. What happens here is that you check yourself into a facility, are placed under anesthesia or are heavily sedated, and are injected with opiate antagonists (such as Naltrexone), that are supposed to "flush" the opiates from your system and block withdrawal symptoms. There is also what is called a "naltrexone implant" that will block opiates from working in your system. The only suggestion with regards to trying these methods is to do thorough research on both the methods and the particular facility before moving forward. There is no conclusive evidence that these are safe and effective treatments. In fact, there have been some patients with very negative experiences, so tread carefully.

Another consideration with methadone is the recommendation of tapering. Some are able to do this successfully and then quit "cold turkey" from a much lower level methadone, lessening the withdrawal symptoms. If you do decide to try tapering with methadone, check out the hard rules for tapering listed in the first section of the book and be sure to stick to them. It is highly recommended that you taper your dose of methadone over as long a period as you are able before you stop taking it completely. A general guide is to lower your dose anywhere from 2mg-5mg per month until you are down to zero. You can do this faster if you must, but remember that everyone's body is different and what may be an easy detox and taper for one person could be very difficult for someone else. Regardless, you will still need to prepare for the eventual withdrawal symptoms.

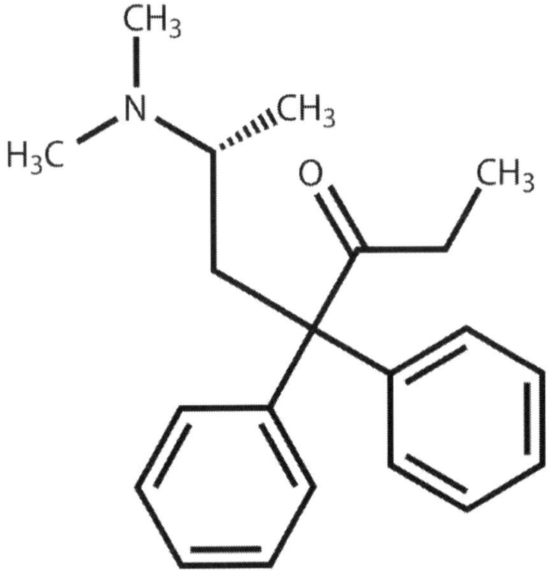

## What to Expect With Methadone Withdrawal at Home

Methadone withdrawal actually shares many symptoms with a (very) bad case of the flu. Expect that you will lose your appetite, feel like sleeping or just be run down and suffer from general feelings of illness. Onset of symptoms may not appear for 48 hours or more because of the long half life of the drug and the amount that has built up in your system. The "acute phase" of detox from methadone can last up to 14 days, with the worst part being over in less than 7 days, depending on the dosage and frequency taken. Methadone withdrawal symptoms are characterized by:

- watery eyes
- runny nose
- anxiety
- insomnia
- dilated pupils
- gooseflesh
- muscle aches and joint pain
- abdominal cramps
- nausea and vomiting
- diarrhea
- hot and cold flashes

The post-acute withdrawal symptoms of insomnia, fatigue and mild anxiety can last for many months after stopping taking the drug. This is the period of time in which the body's opiate receptors heal and the body learns to produce its own endorphins again. You can help this along through moderate exercise and good nutrition, as well as seeking out some sort of a support network (see final chapters of book on this).

## Preparation for Methadone Detox at Home

*Believe that life is worth living and your belief will help create the fact. -William James*

If you are planning to detox from methadone at home, be sure to review the general home detox guide in the first chapter that applies to all home detox procedures. Aside from that, you'll need to make some special preparations with respect to detoxing from methadone at home.

### Prepare the Environment

Again, one of the reasons that you are likely choosing to do this at home instead of in an institution is "comfort". If so, be sure that you have everything on hand to make your stay as comfortable, and safe, as possible. Detoxing from methadone and methadone withdrawal can actually last quite a long time so you'll want to make plans to be away from work or school for at least a week if you can. You will be home for the duration so have something to keep yourself busy, whether it be books, movies, games, etc. Also, get rid of all drugs in the home. This should be a no brainer but it needs to be said. This is no joke. There is no "saving some for an emergency". If you've gone through the exercise in which you address "Why you are doing this", there shouldn't be much resistance here. Just get rid of them - toss them or give them away immediately. Trust me - you will not be able to resist the temptation once the withdrawal symptoms and cravings set in.

## Support

Did you line up a family member or friend to come and stay with you? If not, do so now. This needs to happen from at least Day 2 (preferably from the beginning), as any opiate detox can by psychologically very difficult. Probably after Day 6 or so, you will be in the clear and they can just check on you, but this will vary on a case by case basis.

Also, try to get an appointment with your family physician and request a prescription for a long-acting Benzo such as Valium or Librium. Let your physician know what you are trying to do and that you simply want to take a reducing dose of this medication over the course of several days to lessen the withdrawal symptoms. (see "Opiate Detox" chapter for a sample schedule). Other prescription medications that may be of assistance are:

- **Clonidine** - 01. or 0.2 mg, 2-3x per day to help ease withdrawal symptoms.

If you are unable to get prescription medication to ease the symptoms, you can still find some comfort with over-the-counter medicines, supplements, vitamins and diet.

Here are some over-the-counter medications that you'll want to pick up and their uses:

- **Imodium (Loperamide)** - This is a must-have. It can help with the diarrhea that is likely to come and the gastrointestinal symptoms. Also, it is structurally similar to Demerol and can ease the overall harshness of the detox.
- **Benadryl (Diphenhydramine)** - This is another highly recommended. This can help with anxiety, restlessness, insomnia and the cold-like symptoms. Take 25-50 mgs every 6 hours as needed.
- **Topical Creams containing Methyl Salicylate (Bengay, Icy Hot)** - for joint and muscle pain.

- **Calcium Carbonate (Tums)** - 1 to 2 tablets every 8 hours for abdominal pain and indigestion.
- **OTC Pain Reliever** such as Tylenol, Aleve, Aspirin or Ibuprofen.

As for vitamins and supplements, here are the things that you'll want to consider picking up if your budget allows (you had money for your drugs, didn't you?). Simply stick with the recommended dosages for all of these:

- Vitamin B6 caps
- Vitamin C
- Vitamin E
- Calcium

- Magnesium
- L-Glutamine
- Melatonin
- Valerian Root
- Passion Flower
- Milk Thistle

**If you can find the 1st five of these in a good multi-vitamin, that's fine too.

**Diet**

When we don't feel well, or are anticipating not feeling well, it's tempting to grab a bunch of "comfort foods" and sustain ourselves on them. In this case, that would be a mistake. Chips and cookies are not going to give our liver the nutrients that it needs as it is over-working to detoxify our body from these mass amounts of opiates that have built up in it. You'll want to reduce the load on your liver by minimizing the processed foods and saturated fats that you put in your body. Stay away from canned and processed foods, as well as candy and other sugar-heavy foods. If you're not feeling well, it's ok to eat in small amounts but when you do eat something, eat the right things and stock up on some of this stuff:

- Fiber-rich fruits and vegetables
- Healthy proteins from chicken, fish and eggs
- Plant proteins such as beans and peas
- Healthy fats from fish
- Bland soup or broth
- Nuts, seeds, extra virgin olive oil

Also, fluid intake is critical. Drink lots of water. Stay away from soda and coffee for at least 3 weeks. Your sleep patterns will already be disturbed and these are not going to help. Green tea is also ok to drink and is good for its antioxidants and anti inflammatory properties. Cranberry juice is also a great drink that has some natural sugars and a lot of benefits. It's ok to have a few sports drinks for flavor but stick mostly to good old fashioned water - and lots of it.

## Other Activities

When the detox and withdrawal process starts, there is nothing else to do but ride it out and take it day by day or, if necessary, hour by hour. Don't forget to sleep when you are able, which for some people may be all the time, and to simply keep yourself occupied when you aren't. If you are prepared, you have some movies, books or something else to keep yourself busy for next several days during the periods that you are unable to sleep. Use hot and cool baths to get comfortable as needed and as often as you like. If you have access to a swimming pool or hot tub and it helps, don't think twice about sitting in there all day long if you need to. Also, consider that a small amount exercise can go a long way in making you feel better. Those cramped muscles can be stretched and some endorphins can be released, which is so very important to your well-being. This can be as simple as a 10 minute walk once per day. Finally, don't be too hard on yourself and don't forget why you are doing this. Hopefully you went through some sort of exercise in self examination before beginning this process so that you know why it is that you are getting off of methadone and what positive things you hope to gain from a life without it.

## After Methadone Detox

The acute phase of methadone withdrawal can be over in as little as 5-7 days. That's just it though, the withdrawal phase and the toxins leaving your body. No doubt this wasn't fun but all of that suffering would be for nothing if you were to walk right back out into the "real world" and resume use. This is an ongoing issue with opiate and methadone addiction and the list of things that methadone addicts simply do not understand include:

Addiction is a bona fide disease (Read the Disease Chapter - this is important)
Additional help or treatment is available and probably recommended
Finding a good support network is critical to remaining clean long term

Otherwise, you have successfully detoxed from methadone at home. Maybe this wasn't the first time. Regardless, it likely wasn't fun and not something that you would want to repeat or even do over and over again. If that's the case, please check out those final chapters in the book and the Resource Section before moving on.

# Marijuana Detox at Home

*Be miserable. Or motivate yourself. Whatever has to be done, it's always your choice. -Wayne Dyer*

It's easy for many to downplay marijuana use and its effects. Heck, it's being legalized left and right, so how can it be dangerous, right? Hint: Alcohol is legal too. Regardless, the fact is that regular or heavy use of marijuana can cause adverse affects on work or school performance and on personal relationships. In the past, it was also thought that marijuana was not an addictive substance but repeated studies have put that notion to bed and also proven that there are, in fact, adverse affects to the dependant user who quits using. Whether the cause of the symptoms are physical or psychological, many of the results are physical and need to be managed.

Marijuana is currently the 3rd most popular recreational drug in the U.S., trailing only tobacco and alcohol, and has been used by nearly 100 million Americans. According to U.S. government surveys, nearly 14 million Americans use the drug regularly. The plant, Cannabis sativa, contains more than 400 chemicals, including delta-9-tetrahydrocannabinaol (THC), the plant's main psychoactive chemical. THC is known to affect the brain's short term memory as well as having an effect on motor coordination, anxiety and an increased heart rate. The initial effects created by the THC may wear off after an hour or two but the chemicals will remain in your body for much longer. This is dependent on the half life of the particular strain (potency) of marijuana and amount that you consume.

Another thing to consider is that the potency of marijuana has increased exponentially over the years. What was a "great strain" in 1972 with THC levels of 3% is child's play today, where some specially grown plants have levels as high as 15%. Unlike most other drugs, including alcohol, THC is stored in the fat cells and therefore takes much longer to completely clear the body. This means that some parts of the body will continue to retain THC even after a couple of months from stopping, as opposed to a few days or weeks for water soluble drugs. Regardless, weed detox and marijuana withdrawal at home are manageable with proper preparations.

## What to Expect With Marijuana Withdrawal

If you have been a regular and/or heavy user of marijuana and have decided to quit, expect to feel some adverse effects. Everyone is different, though. What may result in mild irritation and discomfort for one person could be quite an ordeal for someone else. Another thing to consider as you go into this are any co-concurring physical or mental disorders that may need to be managed. Many people use marijuana to self-medicate for both physical and psychological issues. If you are making the choice to stop doing this, consider how you will be managing those issues otherwise. While "tapering" is always a possibility with marijuana, it will likely be difficult for a heavy or regular user to regulate their use enough to be able to do this successfully. Once you do stop using, expect the onset of symptoms to appear within 12-24 hours and to include:

- Insomnia
- Restlessness
- Depression
- Irritability
- Headaches
- Anxiety
- Stomach Pain
- Loss of appetite
- Nausea, diarrhea
- Cough
- Excess sweating
- Vivid dreams

The insomnia is generally what bothers most people and we'll address this more in the next section. This, unfortunately can last anywhere from a week to several months. Depression and anxiety are also common issues to contend with. These will also fade with time, anywhere from a few weeks to several months.

None of these sound like a walk in the park, do they? The psychological effect of taking away a substance that you used on regular, and likely heavy, basis is acute and something that you need to be prepared for. Detox from marijuana needs to be focused primarily on managing mood and cravings more than anything else. If you can get through the initial phase of withdrawals and cravings, with solid reminders of why you are doing this and what sorts of benefits you stand gain, you have a much greater chance of success. There are still other preparations that you can make beforehand to make your detox much more comfortable.

## Preparation for Detoxing From Marijuana at Home

*With the new day comes new strength and new thoughts. -Eleanor Roosevelt*

If you are planning to detox from marijuana at home, be sure to review the general home detox guide in the first chapter that applies to all home detox procedures. Aside from that, you'll need to make some special preparations with respect to detoxing from marijuana at home.

### Prepare the Environment

A few of the reasons that you are likely choosing to do this at home instead of in a detox facility or hospital are privacy and "comfort". If so, be sure that you have everything on hand to make your stay as comfortable, and safe, as possible. Detoxing from marijuana and its withdrawal doesn't last as long as some others and you may very well be able to take care of some of your "normal" activities while this is going on. Again, everyone is different and this could be a cake walk for you but prepare for it not to be. It's quite possible that you will be home for the duration so have something to keep yourself busy, whether it be books, movies, games, etc. Also, get rid of all of the drugs in the home. This should be a no brainer but it needs to be said. This is no joke. There is no "saving some for a special occasion" or "just in case". If you've gone through the exercise in which you address "Why you are doing this", there shouldn't be much resistance here. Just get rid of it - toss it or give it away immediately. Trust me - you will not be able to resist the temptation once the craving and withdrawal symptoms set in. Your success or failure could hinge on this single step.

**Support**

Did you line up a family member or friend to come and stay with you? If not, consider doing this now. You may not be physically in dire straits but the "mental game" is going to require that someone is there and in your corner. This needs to happen from Day 1, as marijuana detox can by psychologically very difficult. Probably after Day 3 or 4, you will be in the clear and they can just check on you daily, but this will vary on a case by case basis.

There really are not any prescription medications that are specifically recommended to help with marijuana detox. If you have an incredibly understanding physician you may wish to ask for a small quantity of long-acting benzos (such as Valium) to take over the course of 5-6 days to help with the anxiety if it is acute (see opiate detox for dosages). Otherwise, this isn't necessary and there are not any other recommended prescriptions for a home detox. Regardless, you can still find some comfort with over-the-counter medicines, supplements, vitamins and diet.

Here are some over-the-counter medications that you'll want to pick up and their uses:

- **Benadryl (Diphenhydramine)** - This one is recommended. This can help with anxiety, restlessness, and insomnia. Take 25-50 mgs every 6 hours as needed.
- **Calcium Carbonate (Tums)** - 1 to 2 tablets every 8 hours for abdominal pain and indigestion.
- **OTC Pain Reliever** such as Tylenol, Aleve, Aspirin or Ibuprofen for headaches.

As for vitamins and supplements, here are the things that you'll want to consider picking up if your budget allows (you had money for your drugs, didn't you?). Simply stick with the recommended dosages for all of these:

- Vitamin B

- Vitamin C
- Vitamin E
- Calcium
- Magnesium
- Thiamin
- Niacin
- L-Glutamine
- Milk Thistle (helps with liver repair)
- Valerian Root (very helpful for insomnia)
- Passion Flower

**If you can find the 1st five of these in a good multi-vitamin, that's fine too.

**Diet**

While there may be periods of time where you have no or little appetite, diet is critical and having the right foods and beverages on hand is very important. You'll want to pick up lots of fruits and vegetables, whether they are your favorites or not. This is about replacing the toxins that are leaving your body with good things that are going to make you feel better, and Ice Cream or Doritos aren't going to cut it. Berries are an excellent snack that contain natural sugar, which is something that ex-users tend to crave. Oats are also good for controlling blood sugar and serve as a relaxant. Bananas are great for lifting mood and a great source of energy, fiber and potassium. Also pick up some food that is high in protein, like chicken, fish or even peanut butter. When you do eat, it's ok to only eat in small portions. Don't force yourself to eat large meals as this isn't necessary.

Finally, the intake of fluids cannot be stressed enough. It's crucial that you drink moderate to large amounts of water. Do not consume more than 2 quarts in an hour, however. It is ok to mix in a few sports drinks for flavor but try to stick primarily to water for fluid intake. You may also want to add some cranberry juice to the mix as it helps to purify and cleanse the body. Staying hydrated will help the withdrawal symptoms be less severe and allow the toxins to flush out of your system more quickly. Stay away from caffeinated drinks like coffee and tea. Your sleep patterns will already be very disturbed. These drinks will only exacerbate that and will not help to keep you hydrated.

**Other Activities**

Other things you'll want to do during detox to ease symptoms include taking frequent baths, or sitting in a pool if you have one available as this can help the emotions as well as the body. The water temperature should really be to your comfort - whatever is going to make you feel better and more comfortable at that moment. It could be the complete opposite just a little while later. Mild exercise, such as stretching and going for a short walk, may also help with circulation and anxiety through the release of endorphins. Releasing these natural "feel good" neurotransmitters can help to ease feelings of depression and anxiety. Rest when you are able and keep your mind busy when you aren't. Don't worry about what time it is or isn't. Your body clock isn't going to be right for quite some time so sleep when you can. When you can't sleep, keep your mind occupied with those books or movies that you have on hand and planning that wonderful new life free from drugs that you have in front of you.

## After Marijuana Detox

After about 36 hours, you will be generally uncomfortable and mostly irritable for the rest of the week. Continue with your detox routine, healthy diet, vitamins, supplements, moderate exercise and intermittent sleep. In less than a week, you should be ready to resume some "normal" activities provided they are not too stressful. What's most important to note here is that you've simply detoxed from weed, nothing else. You have successfully gotten some of the toxins out of your system but, unless you make some other changes in your life, you will more than likely end up right back where you were a week ago - or worse. To prevent this from happening requires several things:

Learn that addiction is a bona fide disease (Read the Disease Chapter - this is important)
Additional help or treatment is available and probably recommended
Finding a good support network is critical to remaining clean long term

Marijuana addiction is real and robs those affected of their initiative, clouds emotions and dulls clarity. Marijuana is associated with an increased risk for a number of different cancers, and also with a substantially increased likelihood towards certain psychiatric disorders. Quitting is tough and anyone who takes steps to do so should be commended. If you have taken these steps, you have successfully detoxed from marijuana at home. It likely wasn't fun and not something that you would want to repeat or even do over and over again. If that's the case, please check out those final chapters in the book and the Resource Section before moving on.

# Detoxing from Drugs at Home - Other Drugs

It would be nearly impossible to cover every single drug that you may want to, or need to, detox from in a single book. However, we have covered the main classes of drugs so far and the ones that people seem to get into the most trouble with. Before we wrap this up, however, there are still a few that bear some attention due to their unique classes, widespread abuse and confusion as to how to safely get off of them in a home environment. So, here we're going to cover what you need to know about addiction and withdrawal from Barbiturates, Sedatives (Ambien), Ecstasy and GHB.

# Barbiturate Addiction and Withdrawal Information

*Learn from the past, set vivid, detailed goals for the future, and live in the only moment of time over which you have any control: now. -Denis Waitley*

## The Nature of Barbiturate Addiction

Barbiturates were first introduced for medical use in the early 1900's and, since that time, more than 2,500 forms have been synthesized. At the height of their popularity, about 50 were marketed for human use, with today about a dozen still in circulation. Originally developed for use as sedatives, anesthetics and anti-convulsants, barbiturates became popular for recreational use in the 1950s and 1960s. These drugs produce a wide spectrum of central nervous system depression, from mild sedation to coma, and have been found to be both addictive and highly prone to overdose.

The difference in the various barbiturates lies in their half life, how quickly they produce an effect and how long that effect lasts. Very short acting barbiturates are often used as anesthetics. Drug abusers seem to prefer the medium to shorter-acting drugs that are Schedule II, such as amobarbital (Amytal), pentobarbital (Nembutal), secobarbital (Seconal), and Tuinal (an amobarbital/secobarbital combination product). Other short and intermediate-acting barbiturates are in Schedule III and include butalbital (Fiorina), butabarbital (Butisol), talbutal (Lotusate), and aprobarbital (Alurate). Many of these drugs have street names as well, such as:

- Amobarbital (downers, blue heavens, blue velvet, blue devils)
- Pentobarbital (nembies, yellow jackets, abbots, mexican yellows)
- Phenobarbital (purple hearts, goof balls)
- Secobarbital (reds, red birds, red devils, lilly, F-40s, pinks, pink ladies)
- Tuinal (rainbows, reds & blues, tooies, double trouble, gorilla pills, F66s)

Those who abuse barbiturates state that they feel "euphoric" feelings and weightlessness. Even though they come in pill form, common methods for using these drugs are orally, snorting or injecting. Depending on the level of use and other factors, barbiturate withdrawal may need to be monitored in a medical setting. Otherwise, all other things being equal and with proper planning, you may be able to manage this at home.

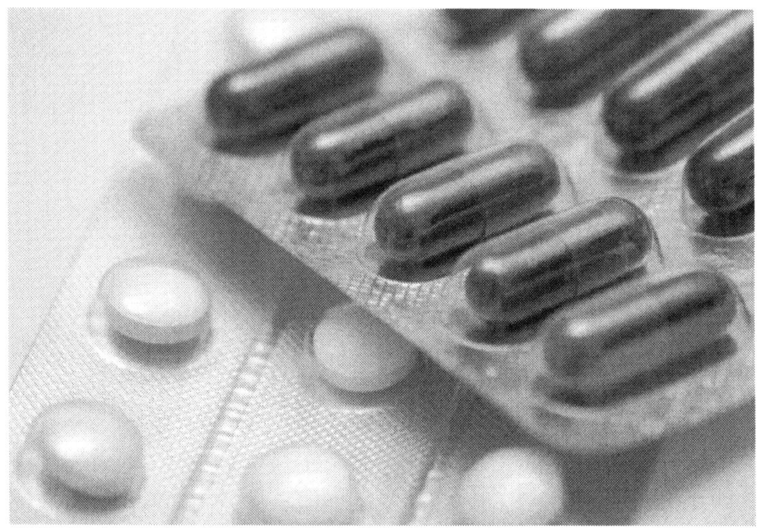

## Managing Barbiturate Withdrawal at Home

Barbiturate withdrawal can be difficult, particularly if you have been on high doses of the pills for a prolonged period of time. If you are able to set up some sort of tapering schedule for yourself, and stick to it, this would be best. Refer back to our general guide to tapering at the beginning of the book on how to taper off of a drug. If you are not able to taper and need to stop "cold turkey", you can likely manage the withdrawal at home provided you meet several criteria:

- Have a safe, comfortable place to go through withdrawal symptoms, away from temptation.
- Not have a history of severe withdrawal symptoms or of trying and failing to withdraw at home.
- You have no co-occurring medical or psychiatric conditions that would require close observation during this period.

Because most of these drugs are fairly short-acting, expect to start feeling some with barbiturate withdrawal symptoms within 4-6 hours of the last dose. Symptoms that you are likely to experience include:

- Anxiety, restlessness
- Nausea
- Excessive sweating
- Tremors
- Insomnia
- Hallucinations

In extreme cases, seizures are possible and can present in the 2nd to 3rd day. If withdrawal symptoms seem severe and are too much to take (have another person there to be the judge), be sure to seek medical attention immediately. Generally, symptoms are much more mild by day 7 or before.

It is important that you make proper preparations for a detox from barbiturates by having the right support and supplies on hand. If you haven't lined up someone to stay with you, do this now. You really need someone staying with you from Day 1 with barbiturates as the symptoms start right away and can last for quite a few days. Don't expect to go to work or probably anyplace while this is going on so have some things on hand to keep you occupied during the times that you are unable to sleep.

If you haven't set up an appointment with your physician to discuss your plans, also do this now. A long-acting Benzo (like Valium) can be a big help in detoxing from barbiturates. This is something that you will be on for a week, at the most, and on a reducing dose to deal with anxiety and ease some of the other withdrawal symptoms. See the "Opiate Detox" chapter for a sample schedule. If you are unable to get a prescription, that's ok. You can still find some comfort with over-the-counter medicines, supplements, vitamins and diet.

Here are some over-the-counter medications that you'll want to pick up and their uses:

- **Benadryl (Diphenhydramine)** - This one is recommended. This can help with anxiety, restlessness, and insomnia. Take 25-50 mgs every 6 hours as needed.
- **Calcium Carbonate (Tums)** - 1 to 2 tablets every 8 hours for abdominal pain and indigestion.
- **OTC Pain Reliever** such as Tylenol, Aleve, Aspirin or Ibuprofen for headaches.

As for vitamins and supplements, here are the things that you'll want to consider picking up if your budget allows (you had money for your drugs, didn't you?). Simply stick with the recommended dosages for all of these:

- Vitamin B
- Vitamin C
- Vitamin E

- Calcium
- Magnesium
- Thiamin
- Niacin
- L-Glutamine
- Milk Thistle (helps with liver repair)
- Valerian Root (very helpful for insomnia)
- Passion Flower

**If you can find the 1st five of these in a good multi-vitamin, that's fine too.

Aside from these things, how you treat your body from this point forward also has a lot to do with how the rest of your detox is going to go for you. While there may be periods of time where you have no or little appetite, diet is critical and having the right foods and beverages on hand is very important. You'll want to pick up lots of fruits and vegetables, whether they are your favorites or not. This is about replacing the toxins that are leaving your body with good things that are going to make you feel better, and Ice Cream or Doritos aren't going to cut it. Oats are also good for controlling blood sugar and serve as a relaxant. Bananas are great for lifting mood and a great source of energy, fiber and potassium. Also pick up some food that is high in protein, like chicken, fish or even peanut butter. When you do eat, it's ok to only eat in small portions. Don't force yourself to eat large meals as this isn't necessary.

The intake of fluids cannot be stressed enough. It's crucial that you drink moderate to large amounts of water. Do not consume more than 2 quarts in an hour, however. It is ok to mix in a few sports drinks for flavor but try to stick primarily to water for fluid intake. You may also want to add some cranberry juice to the mix as it helps to purify and cleanse the body. Staying hydrated will help the withdrawal symptoms be less severe and allow the toxins to flush out of your system more quickly. Stay away from caffeinated drinks like coffee and tea. Your sleep patterns will already be very disturbed. These drinks will only exacerbate that and will not help to keep you hydrated.

Finally, other things you'll want to do during barbiturate withdrawal to ease symptoms include taking frequent baths as this can help the emotions as well as the body. The water temperature should really be to your comfort - whatever is going to make you feel better and more comfortable at that moment. It could be the complete opposite just a little while later. Mild exercise, such as stretching and going for a short walk, may also help with circulation and anxiety through the release of endorphins. Releasing these natural "feel good" neurotransmitters can help to ease feelings of depression and anxiety. Rest when you are able and keep your mind busy when you aren't. When you can't sleep, keep your mind occupied with those books or movies that you have on hand and planning that wonderful new life free from drugs that you have in front of you.

## Ambien Addiction and Withdrawal Information

*At fifteen life had taught me undeniably that surrender, in its place, was as honorable as resistance, especially if one had no choice. -Maya Angelou*

### The Nature of Ambien Addiction

Ambien is America's most popular sleeping pill. The National Survey on Drug Use and Health found that over half a million people are currently abusing Ambien and other sedatives. According to the United States Mental Health Department, over 17,000 emergency-room visits each year are attributed to the misuse or overdose of Ambien. It works great for many people that have sleep disorders yet, what many don't realize is that the manufacturer recommends that it not be used for longer than 7 to 10 days. Take it longer than this and you are at risk for Ambien addiction and Ambien is highly addictive. What happens for many is that they take the drug way beyond this "short term" period, users develop a tolerance and take more than prescribed, and "rebound insomnia" may develop which creates an endless cycle of taking more of the drug for less and less effect.

Most people don't "plan" to become addicted to one drug or another but Ambien addiction is one that does grab a lot of people out of left field because it is sudden and many aren't told the risks when it is first prescribed. Other harmful effects of the drug are the side effects of "retrograde amnesia", where users forget things that happened just before or after the drug is taken, and the masking of underlying issues for which the drug was taken in the first place. It's not surprising that, once people find out that they are in fact "addicted" to this little sleeping pill, they start searching for ways to get free from it. Depending on the level of use and other factors, Ambien withdrawal may need to be monitored in a medical setting. Otherwise, all other things being equal and with proper planning, you may be able to manage this at home.

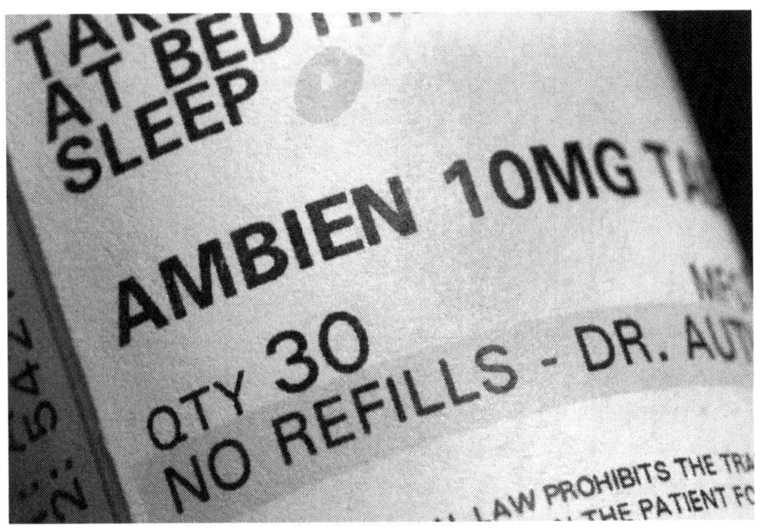
SLEEP
AMBIEN 10MG
QTY 30
NO REFILLS - DR.
LAW PROHIBITS THE
THE PATIENT

## Managing Ambien Withdrawal at Home

Ambien withdrawal can be difficult, particularly if you have been on high doses of the pills for a prolonged period of time. If you are able to set up some sort of tapering schedule for yourself, and stick to it, this would be best. Refer back to our general guide to tapering at the beginning of the book on how to taper off of a drug. If you are not able to taper and need to stop "cold turkey", you can likely manage the withdrawal at home provided you meet several criteria:

- Have a safe, comfortable place to go through withdrawal symptoms, away from temptation.
- Not have a history of severe withdrawal symptoms or of trying and failing to withdraw at home.
- You have no co-occurring medical or psychiatric conditions that would require close observation during this period.

Because Ambien is fairly short-acting, expect to start feeling some with withdrawal symptoms within 14-16 hours of the last dose, or within a few hours of missing your first one. Symptoms that you are likely to experience include:

- Anxiety
- Severe insomnia
- Depression
- Nausea, vomiting
- Sweating
- Confusion
- Stomach pains, muscle cramps
- Hallucinations

In extreme cases, seizures are possible, yet rare. If withdrawal symptoms seem severe and are too much to take (have another person there to be the judge), be sure to seek medical attention immediately. Generally, symptoms are much more mild by day 5 or before and detox from Ambien has not been found to be life threatening.

It is important that you make proper preparations for a detox from Ambien by having the right support and supplies on hand. If you haven't lined up someone to stay with you, do this now. You really need someone staying with you from Day 1 with sedatives as the symptoms start right away and can last for quite a few days. Don't expect to go to work or probably anyplace while this is going on so have some things on hand to keep you occupied during the times that you are unable to sleep.

If you haven't set up an appointment with your physician to discuss your plans, also do this now. A long-acting Benzo (like Valium) can be a big help in detoxing from sedatives. This is something that you will be on for a week, at the most, and on a reducing dose to deal with anxiety and ease some of the other withdrawal symptoms. See the "Opiate Detox" chapter for a sample schedule. If you are unable to get a prescription, that's ok. You can still find some comfort with over-the-counter medicines, supplements, vitamins and diet.

Here are some over-the-counter medications that you'll want to pick up and their uses:

- **Benadryl (Diphenhydramine)** - This one is recommended. This can help with anxiety, restlessness, and insomnia. Take 25-50 mgs every 6 hours as needed.
- **Calcium Carbonate (Tums)** - 1 to 2 tablets every 8 hours for abdominal pain and indigestion.
- **OTC Pain Reliever** such as Tylenol, Aleve, Aspirin or Ibuprofen for headaches.

As for vitamins and supplements, here are the things that you'll want to consider picking up if your budget allows (you had money for your drugs, didn't you?). Simply stick with the recommended dosages for all of these:

- Vitamin B
- Vitamin C
- Vitamin E
- Calcium
- Magnesium
- Thiamin
- Niacin
- L-Glutamine
- Milk Thistle (helps with liver repair)
- Valerian Root (very helpful for insomnia)
- Passion Flower

**If you can find the 1st five of these in a good multi-vitamin, that's fine too.

Aside from these things, how you treat your body from this point forward also has a lot to do with how the rest of your detox is going to go for you. While there may be periods of time where you have no or little appetite, diet is critical and having the right foods and beverages on hand is very important. You'll want to pick up lots of fruits and vegetables, whether they are your favorites or not. This is about replacing the toxins that are leaving your body with good things that are going to make you feel better, and Ice Cream or Doritos aren't going to cut it. Oats are also good for controlling blood sugar and serve as a relaxant. Bananas are great for lifting mood and a great source of energy, fiber and potassium. Also pick up some food that is high in protein, like chicken, fish or even peanut butter. When you do eat, it's ok to only eat in small portions. Don't force yourself to eat large meals as this isn't necessary.

The intake of fluids cannot be stressed enough. It's crucial that you drink moderate to large amounts of water. Do not consume more than 2 quarts in an hour, however. It is ok to mix in a few sports drinks for flavor but try to stick primarily to water for fluid intake. You may also wish to add some cranberry juice to the mix as it helps to purify and cleanse the body. Staying hydrated will help the withdrawal symptoms be less severe and allow the toxins to flush out of your system more quickly. Stay away from caffeinated drinks like coffee and tea. Your sleep patterns will already be very disturbed. These drinks will only exacerbate that and will not help to keep you hydrated.

Finally, other things you'll want to do during Ambien withdrawal to ease symptoms include taking frequent baths as this can help the emotions as well as the body. The water temperature should really be to your comfort - whatever is going to make you feel better and more comfortable at that moment. It could be the complete opposite just a little while later. Mild exercise, such as stretching and going for a short walk, may also help with circulation and anxiety through the release of endorphins. Releasing these natural "feel good" neurotransmitters can help to ease feelings of depression and anxiety. Rest when you are able and keep your mind busy when you aren't. When you can't sleep, keep your mind occupied with those books or movies that you have on hand and planning that wonderful new life free from drugs that you have in front of you.

# Ecstasy Addiction and Withdrawal Information

*You never find yourself until you face the truth. -Pearl Bailey*

## Breaking Free From Ecstasy Addiction

Ecstasy (also known as MDMA, X, and 3,4-methylenedioxymethamphetamine) is a popular synthetic “club drug” that creates a hallucinogenic effect similar to the “high” that results from mescaline. According to the National Institute on Drug Abuse (NIDA) the effects of Ecstasy include “energy, euphoria, emotional warmth, and distortions in time, perception, and tactile experiences.” Ecstasy was at first popular among adolescents and young adults in the nightclub scene or at "raves" (long late-night dance parties), but the drug now affects a broader range of users. (For everything you ever wanted to know about this particular drug, check out my book "Who is Molly?"). Taken orally, usually as a capsule or tablet, effects generally last 3 to 6 hours, though it is not uncommon for users to re-dose when effects start to wane. It is also common to take MDMA with other drugs, such as cocaine, meth, GHB and even Viagra.

Ecstasy acts by increasing the activity of three neurotransmitters: dopamine, serotonin and norepinephrine. The release of large amounts of serotonin, which influences mood, have a lot to do with the emotional and "pro-social" effects of the drug. This surge, however, depletes the brain of important chemicals, causing negative after-effects such as confusion, depression, sleep problems, anxiety and drug craving. Other physical effects can include muscle tension, involuntary teeth-clenching, nausea, blurred vision, faintness, and chills or sweating. No wonder that some people find that taking regular doses of the drug serves them better and they end up dependent upon it.

## Managing Ecstasy Withdrawal at Home

If you have become dependent on ecstasy and wish to break free, the good news is that ecstasy detox itself is not life threatening. You will most certainly experience some unpleasant symptoms but, provided you are able to meet a few simple criteria and can make some simple preparations, you should not have any problem managing this at home. Also, ecstasy is not something that you "taper" or wean yourself off of. There is no benefit to doing this and it may cause more harm. You simply need to stop taking it and deal with the withdrawal symptoms until they pass. So, detoxing from MDMA at home is feasible provided you can meet these simple criteria:

- Have a safe, comfortable place to go through withdrawal symptoms, away from temptation.
- Not have a history of severe withdrawal symptoms or of trying and failing to withdraw at home.
- You have no co-occurring medical or psychiatric conditions that would require close observation during this period.

The onset of ecstasy withdrawal symptoms is going to vary wildly depending on your level of use - ie - how much you took and how often. For example, if you were taking MDMA around the clock, expect symptoms to start within 4-6 hours of missing your first dose. Symptoms that you are likely to experience include:

- Anxiety
- Insomnia
- Depression
- Irritability
- Memory problems
- Mood fluctuations

Also, because the ecstasy found in clubs is rarely 100% pure, you may have a concurrent addiction to some type of amphetamine-like substance that was mixed in (or "cut") with your MDMA. In this case, you will also experience some "Amphetamine Withdrawal" symptoms and can take a look at the chapter dealing with those to get a better idea on how to manage them. If withdrawal symptoms seem severe and are too much to take (have another person there to be the judge), be sure to seek medical attention immediately. Generally, symptoms are much more mild by day 5 or before and detox from ecstasy has not been found to be life threatening.

What is important to realize with Ecstasy withdrawal is that some level or form of symptoms can be felt for a very long time after you stop taking the drug - sometimes months or even years. Also, in the case of MDMA a lot of damage could have been done both physically and psychologically, sometimes permanent. Increases in heart rate and blood pressure are a special risk for people with circulatory or heart disease. "The serotonin system, which is compromised by MDMA, is fundamental to the brain's integration of information and emotion," says Dr. Alan I. Leshner, director of the National Institute on Drug Abuse (NIDA). "At the very least, people who take MDMA, even just a few times, are risking long-term, perhaps permanent, problems with learning and memory." While many issues can be repaired over time, it's important to stop use as soon as possible and deal with ecstasy detox in the safest and most responsible manner.

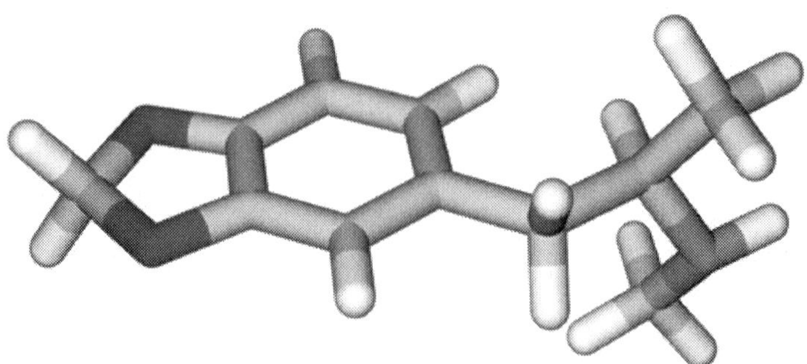

It is important that you make proper preparations for a detox from ecstasy by having the right support and supplies on hand. If you haven't lined up someone to stay with you, do this now. You really need someone staying with you from Day 1 with MDMA as the symptoms could start right away, are emotionally taxing and can last for quite a few days. Don't expect to go to work or probably anyplace while this is going on so have some things on hand to keep you occupied during the times that you are unable to sleep.

If you haven't set up an appointment with your physician to discuss your plans, also do this now. A long-acting Benzo (like Valium) can be a big help in detoxing from ecstasy. This is something that you will be on for a week, at the most, and on a reducing dose to deal with anxiety and ease some of the other withdrawal symptoms. See the "Opiate Detox" chapter for a sample schedule. If you are unable to get a prescription, that's ok. You can still find some comfort with over-the-counter medicines, supplements, vitamins and diet.

Here are some over-the-counter medications that you'll want to pick up and their uses:

- **Benadryl (Diphenhydramine)** - This one is recommended. This can help with anxiety, restlessness, and insomnia. Take 25-50 mgs every 6 hours as needed.
- **OTC Pain Reliever** such as Tylenol, Aleve, Aspirin or Ibuprofen for headaches.

As for vitamins and supplements, here are the things that you'll want to consider picking up if your budget allows (you had money for your drugs, didn't you?). Simply stick with the recommended dosages for all of these:

- Vitamin B
- Vitamin C
- Vitamin E
- Calcium

- Magnesium
- Thiamin
- Niacin
- L-Glutamine
- Milk Thistle (helps with liver repair)
- Valerian Root (very helpful for insomnia)
- Passion Flower

**If you can find the 1st five of these in a good multi-vitamin, that's fine too.

Aside from these things, how you treat your body from this point forward also has a lot to do with how the rest of your detox is going to go for you. While there may be periods of time where you have no or little appetite, diet is critical and having the right foods and beverages on hand is very important. You'll want to pick up lots of fruits and vegetables, whether they are your favorites or not. This is about replacing the toxins that are leaving your body with good things that are going to make you feel better, and Ice Cream or Doritos aren't going to cut it. With ecstasy detox, generally your appetite will increase. This is great because chances are you've been starving yourself and are massively undernourished right now. However, make the right choice and put some good things in your body for once. On the flip side, if you're not feeling well, it's ok to eat in small amounts but when you do eat something, eat the right things. Either way, stock up on some of this stuff:

- Fiber-rich fruits and vegetables
- Healthy proteins from chicken, fish and eggs
- Plant proteins such as beans and peas
- Healthy fats from fish
- Nuts, seeds, extra virgin olive oil

The intake of fluids cannot be stressed enough. It's crucial that you drink moderate to large amounts of water. Do not consume more than 2 quarts in an hour, however. It is ok to mix in a few sports drinks for flavor but try to stick primarily to water for fluid intake. You may also wish to add some cranberry juice to the mix as it helps to purify and cleanse the body. Staying hydrated will help the withdrawal symptoms be less severe and allow the toxins to flush out of your system more quickly. Stay away from caffeinated drinks like coffee and tea. Your sleep patterns will already be very disturbed. These drinks will only exacerbate that and will not help to keep you hydrated.

Finally, other things you'll want to do during ecstasy withdrawal to ease symptoms include taking frequent baths as this can help the emotions as well as the body. The water temperature should really be to your comfort - whatever is going to make you feel better and more comfortable at that moment. It could be the complete opposite just a little while later. Mild exercise, such as stretching and going for a short walk, may also help with circulation and anxiety through the release of endorphins. Releasing these natural "feel good" neurotransmitters can help to ease feelings of depression and anxiety. Rest when you are able and keep your mind busy when you aren't. When you can't sleep, keep your mind occupied with those books or movies that you have on hand and planning that wonderful new life free from drugs that you have in front of you.

## GHB Addiction and Withdrawal Information

*Our greatest weakness lies in giving up. The most certain way to succeed is always to try just one more time. -Thomas A. Edison*

### Breaking Free From GHB Addiction

GHB (short for gamma hydroxybutyrate) was first created in 1960 to relieve pain and treat a variety of conditions. Since the 1990s, GHB has become a popular "club drug" that has also been used by body builders to stimulate muscle growth. A sedative typically found in liquid, tablet, capsule or powder form, GHB is colorless and odorless, which has also led to its use as a date rape drug. On the street, GHB is known as Easy Lay, Gamma 10, G, Scoop, Soap, Gook, Liquid X, Liquid Ecstasy, Somatomax, Grievous Bodily Harm, Georgia Home Boy or Natural Sleep-500. Despite being called "liquid ecstasy", it's important to note that GHB is not at all like ecstasy in either its make up, it's action, or its withdrawal symptoms.

In the past, there was a misconception that GHB was a non-addictive substance. This is far from the truth. In fact, heavy regular users of the drug develop a tolerance to its effects, requiring them to take more to achieve the desired results. Not to be underestimated, GHB is a high risk drug for overdose and for dependence. When taken to excess over a period of weeks, both physical and psychological dependence on the drug develop, which will result in a serious list withdrawal symptoms once taken away.

## Managing GHB Withdrawal at Home

GHB withdrawal can be difficult, particularly if you have been on high doses of the drug for a prolonged period of time. If you are able to set up some sort of tapering schedule for yourself, and stick to it, this would be best. Refer back to our general guide to tapering at the beginning of the book on how to taper off of a drug. Tapering is recommended with this drug as a "cold turkey" detox from GHB is considered to be dangerous. Provided that you are able to taper and then can stop from a much lower dose than you are currently taking, you can likely manage the withdrawal at home provided you meet several criteria:

- Have a safe, comfortable place to go through withdrawal symptoms, away from temptation.
- Not have a history of severe withdrawal symptoms or of trying and failing to withdraw at home.
- You have no co-occurring medical or psychiatric conditions that would require close observation during this period.

A single dose of GHB generally only lasts for 1.5-3 hours and then users will sometimes re-dose continually. Because GHB is very short-acting, expect to start feeling some with withdrawal symptoms within 1-6 hours of the last dose having worn off. Symptoms that you are likely to experience include:

- Anxiety
- Panic
- Heavy sweating
- Delirium
- Hallucinations - auditory and visual
- Tremors
- High blood pressure

- Muscle aches and pains

There has been at least one fatality on record from GHB detox, so this is not something to take lightly. If withdrawal symptoms seem severe and are too much to take (have another person there to be the judge), be sure to seek medical attention immediately. Generally, symptoms are much more mild by day 5-6 or before. Detox from GHB can be similar to alcohol detox and detox from sedatives (Benzos) so many of the same treatments may be used in these cases.
It is important that you make proper preparations for a detox from GHB by having the right support and supplies on hand. If you haven't lined up someone to stay with you, do this now. You really need someone staying with you from Day 1 with GHB as the symptoms start right away and can last for quite a few days, anywhere from 5-15 days. Don't expect to go to work or probably anyplace while this is going on so have some things on hand to keep you occupied during the times that you are unable to sleep.

If you haven't set up an appointment with your physician to discuss your plans, also do this now. A long-acting Benzo (like Valium) can be a big help in detoxing from GHB. This is something that you will be on for a week, at the most, and on a reducing dose to deal with anxiety and ease some of the other withdrawal symptoms. More specifically, if you can find an incredibly understanding physician to help you out, this is what you want to put in a request for:

- **Sedative hypnotics** - a small quantity of long-acting Benzos (such as Valium) to take over the course of 5-6 days to help with the anxiety (see opiate detox for dosages).
- **Antipsychotics (Neuroleptics)** - Medications like haloperidol, olanzapine or phenothiazine may be used in the first 1-2 weeks to manage any psychosis symptoms.
- **Antidepressants** - These may be prescribed to help ease symptoms usually experienced in early recovery from GHB.

If you are unable to get a prescription, that's ok. You can still find some comfort with over-the-counter medicines, supplements, vitamins and diet. Here are some over-the-counter medications that you'll want to pick up and their uses:

- **Benadryl (Diphenhydramine)** - This one is recommended. This can help with anxiety, restlessness, and insomnia. Take 25-50 mgs every 6 hours as needed.
- **Calcium Carbonate (Tums)** - 1 to 2 tablets every 8 hours for abdominal pain and indigestion.
- **Topical Creams containing Methyl Salicylate (Bengay, Icy Hot)** - for any joint and muscle pain.
- **OTC Pain Reliever** such as Tylenol, Aleve, Aspirin or Ibuprofen for muscle pain.

As for vitamins and supplements, here are the things that you'll want to consider picking up if your budget allows (you had money for your drugs, didn't you?). Simply stick with the recommended dosages for all of these:

- Vitamin B
- Vitamin C
- Vitamin E
- Calcium
- Magnesium
- Thiamin
- Niacin
- L-Glutamine
- Milk Thistle (helps with liver repair)
- Valerian Root (very helpful for insomnia)
- Passion Flower

**If you can find the 1st five of these in a good multi-vitamin, that's fine too.

Aside from these things, how you treat your body from this point forward also has a lot to do with how the rest of your detox is going to go for you. While there may be periods of time where you have no or little appetite, diet is critical and having the right foods and beverages on hand is very important. You'll want to pick up lots of fruits and vegetables, whether they are your favorites or not. This is about replacing the toxins that are leaving your body with good things that are going to make you feel better, and Ice Cream or Doritos aren't going to cut it. With GHB detox, generally your appetite will increase. This is great because chances are you've been starving yourself and are massively undernourished right now. However, make the right choice and put some good things in your body for once. On the flip side, if you're not feeling well, it's ok to eat in small amounts but when you do eat something, eat the right things. Either way, stock up on some of this stuff:

- Fiber-rich fruits and vegetables
- Healthy proteins from chicken, fish and eggs
- Plant proteins such as beans and peas
- Healthy fats from fish
- Nuts, seeds, extra virgin olive oil

The intake of fluids cannot be stressed enough. It's crucial that you drink moderate to large amounts of water. Do not consume more than 2 quarts in an hour, however. It is ok to mix in a few sports drinks for flavor but try to stick primarily to water for fluid intake. You may also wish to add some cranberry juice to the mix as it helps to purify and cleanse the body. Staying hydrated will help the withdrawal symptoms be less severe and allow the toxins to flush out of your system more quickly. Stay away from caffeinated drinks like coffee and tea. Your sleep patterns will already be very disturbed. These drinks will only exacerbate that and will not help to keep you hydrated.

Finally, other things you'll want to do during GHB withdrawal to ease symptoms include taking frequent baths as this can help the emotions as well as the body. The water temperature should really be to your comfort - whatever is going to make you feel better and more comfortable at that moment. It could be the complete opposite just a little while later. Mild exercise, such as stretching and going for a short walk, may also help with circulation and anxiety through the release of endorphins. Releasing these natural "feel good" neurotransmitters can help to ease feelings of depression and anxiety. Rest when you are able and keep your mind busy when you aren't. When you can't sleep, keep your mind occupied with those books or movies that you have on hand and planning that wonderful new life free from drugs that you have in front of you.

# Life After Detox - Stop the Madness Merry-Go-Round

*If we don't change our direction, we are likely to end up where we are headed. - Ancient Chinese Proverb*

If this is your first go around with a Detox experience, be glad that it's over. Don't stop reading though as there are some important things that you need to consider, some "hard facts" if you will. If you've been through this before, the following will likely not come as much of a surprise to you, yet the reminders may do you some good and, hopefully, send you in the right direction this time. The fact of the matter is that simply getting the drugs and/or alcohol out of our system isn't enough to recover from addiction. Many of us, myself included, have suffered from the delusions that we were simply trapped in a "physical addiction" and, once free, would be able to resume living life just as we had before all of this nonsense started. Wrong! There is an "invisible line" that has been crossed and you will never be able to go back to that "old life". That's the bad news. The good news is that you absolutely can recover from this and lead an even better life than you had ever imagined. Yes, it sounds ridiculous and like a bunch of "hocus pocus" right now, but stick with me here. There is light at the end of the tunnel after a bit more education and self discovery.

OPPORTUNITY
DEAD END

## Understanding that Addiction is a Disease

*It ain't what you don't know that gets you into trouble. It's what you know for sure that just ain't so.* -*Mark Twain*

A fact that most addicts and alcoholics are in the dark about is that they actually have a "disease" and are not simply bad people that can't control themselves. In fact, for over 100 years, alcoholism has been treated as and defined as a "disease". In 1956, the American Medical Association voted to define alcoholism as a disease and, according to the National Institute on Drug Abuse (NIDA), "Addiction is defined as a chronic, relapsing brain disease that is characterized by compulsive drug seeking and use, despite harmful consequences." The American Society of Addiction Medicine (ASAM) also recently revised its definition of addiction to state that: "Addiction is a chronic brain disorder, and not merely a behavioral problem or simply the result of taking the wrong choices". Addiction is now described as a primary disease - not caused by something else, such as a psychiatric or emotional problem. Dr. Michael Miller, former president of ASAM, who oversaw the development of the new definition, said: "At its core, addiction isn't just a social problem or a moral problem or a criminal problem. It's a brain problem whose behaviors manifest in all these other areas. Many behaviors driven by addiction are real problems and sometimes criminal acts. But the disease is about brains, not drugs. It's about underlying neurology, not outward actions."

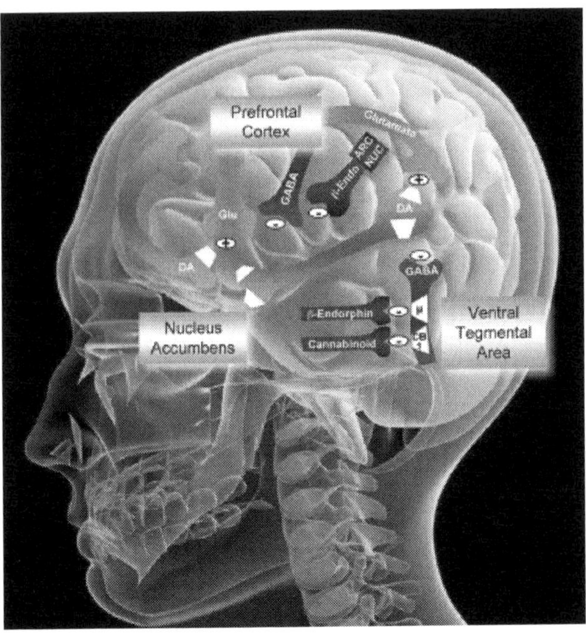


A few additional characteristics of the disease of Addiction (and Alcoholism - same thing) to be aware of are:

**Mental Obsession** - Defined as a thought process over which you have no control. Sounds like fun, right? These maddening urges to use or drink, when many times we know that the results will be disastrous. I always call this the "preoccupation" that I always had with when I would be able to get that next drink or drug - or how I would be able to get more than my "share".

**Chronic Disease** - By chronic, we mean that it is "incurable" (keep reading anyway) and requires long-term treatment. This is a disease that can also result in death if not treated.

**Progressive** - This one is important. (Well, the other two were also.) Addiction and Alcoholism is a subtly progressive disease that gets worse over time - NEVER better. Sometimes, this takes place over such an extended period of time that the addict does not notice the point at which they truly lost control. And, you know what? It doesn't matter. Because as soon as that control is "lost", it can NEVER be regained. EVER. This is where the difficulty and the denial come into play for so many. We remember that time when things were great, fun, easy, controllable and try with all our might, sometimes for entirely too long, to recapture it. It just won't happen.

So what does all of this new-found knowledge mean for the "addicted" or stricken person? Well, the good news is that you're "sick"! Yes, in this case, consider this good news. Think of it in these terms: you no longer need look at yourself as a bad person or an evil person who has screwed up their life and can't control themselves. The truth is that you are a "sick person" who simply needs to take some steps to get well. This is entirely possible and well within your reach if it is something that you want. While there is no cure per se for addiction, or alcoholism, this is a disease that you can recover from and lead a happy, healthy and productive life. However, if you think that you had to do a little bit of self seeking and self discovery before jumping into a detox situation, that was a cake walk. Reaching a point of "surrender" and starting the road to recovery requires that you be willing to honestly take a look at yourself and take some action.

## Am I Really Done With Drugs and Alcohol?

*"If I could drink like a regular person...I'd drink all the time. Therein lies our paradox..."*

Hopefully you asked yourself this question before you put yourself through a home detox. What's important to understand here is that for most of us, drugs and alcohol provided some sort of benefits in the beginning and for potentially a long period of time in our lives. Then, at some point, negative consequences of using and drinking started to accumulate and, either it just wasn't fun anymore, it wasn't working anymore, or the consequences were too painful to want to continue using. Regardless, many of us call this a "bottom" and you should take some time to try to define what your bottom is and how it could (and would) get worse should you continue to use.

Unfortunately, alcoholics and addicts are characterized by extreme arrogance and stubbornness. This is why many of us have multiple "bottoms" - where we stop using and think that we can control our drinking and using so decide to give it another try. I can tell you from experience and from observing countless others that things always get worse and that attempts to control an addiction are, in the end, futile. Sometimes deadly. The fact of the matter is this - we can choose our bottom. This can be it - right now.

ONE WAY
ONE WAY

## Should I Go to Treatment?

*If you want what you've never had, you must do what you've never done.*

Most addicts and alcoholics assume that they have to go to treatment to get better. I did and ended up in an endless stream of rehabs. In fact, if you spend any time in front of the television (most do), then we are taught that in order to "get sober", you have to go to rehab. This isn't necessarily the case and the treatment center industry has seen a recent "boom" in the past few decades as getting sober is now all the rage. So, are these fancy places necessary to start your road to recovery? This is hotly debated and the answer is different for each individual. Many people are able to get clean and sober and stay that way with the help of 12 Step programs alone - no rehab. However, in our fast paced society with all of life's demands, treatment centers certainly have carved out their niche in the "getting sober" process and have some very real value.

It may be that you haven't been given a choice. The edict to "go to rehab" could have been handed down by an employer, a family member, or even a judge. If that's the case, the question has been answered for you. Otherwise, if you are still pondering whether or not to go to treatment, there are several different types of treatment centers to choose from and they certainly do have their benefits if you decide to go.

**Different Types of Treatment Centers**

Choices abound as to what sort of treatment center, if any, is going to be right for you. You will need to decide between Inpatient or Outpatient, Private or Public and, in some cases, Co-Ed or Single Sex treatment centers.

**Inpatient vs Outpatient** - Many people are inclined to select "outpatient" right off the bat because we are also inclined to downplay the seriousness of our situation and the means necessary to recover from it. Some people are able to successfully participate in treatment programs on a part-time basis while continuing to live at home, manage their family lives and keep their jobs. These people are exceptions to the rule, however. There are other outpatient treatment programs that simply have you go to treatment during the day and return to your home (and family) at night. Again, depending on your circumstances, this may be a viable option. For many, and for a lot of reasons, it's not for a lot of people.

Inpatient drug and alcohol treatment is more the norm for quite a few reasons. This option dictates that the individual moves into some sort of dorm-like setting and receives 24/7 care and supervision. Some treatment centers allow for private and semi-private rooms, while others you will essentially take what you are given. Inpatient treatment is the ideal choice for someone who needs a place to focus entirely on their addiction and developing their recovery program.

**Private vs Public** - Regardless of the previous differences, you will run into rehab centers that are both Private and Publicly funded. Different treatment funding sources include:

- Private: Non-profit, or For Profit
- State or Locally Funded
- Low Cost Treatment Centers

- Free Rehabs (Charity Rehabs)

While the Free, Low Cost and Government Funded treatment centers sound great (they are, I got sober in one), it's important to note that many also have long waiting lists. Another difference, although not true in all cases, may be the size of groups in therapy sessions, with smaller groups in Private facilities and larger groups in publicly funded rehabs. Also, do not expect to get into any sort of private or semi-private room in a public facility. In retrospect, being "pampered" did nothing to get me sober. I did find the many waiting lists very disheartening though when I was finally "ready" for this and just couldn't get in anyplace. So, if you are looking at Private treatment centers and possible ways to finance it, consider these:

- **Health Insurance** - most "good" health insurance policies provide for some form of substance abuse treatment. If you have a really good policy, you may be able to get an inpatient treatment program paid for
- **Family Members** - you may already have family members offering to pay to get you sober. I did. I even had friends of family willing to chip in at one point.
- **Sell stock or take money from your 401k** - If you're unemployed, in jail or dead, there will be no "retirement" to save for, right?
- **Home Equity Loan** - If you are lucky enough to still be holding onto your home, consider this.
- **Sell stuff, even your car** - Chances are you have expensive toys you haven't been using because of you've been putting all of your efforts into drinking and drugging. Sell them. You don't need a car if you're not sober. It's a hazard.
- **Substance Abuse Treatment Loan** - Yes, they have these now.

**Co-ed vs Same Sex Treatment Centers** - I've been to both and it didn't make a difference to me either way. However, if you have been the victim of abuse and think that you would feel safer in a same sex facility, by all means, check them out.

## The Pros and Cons of Going to Rehab

When I first started hitting the treatment centers, I didn't see any "Pro's" to this nonsense whatsoever. I did not want to be there, did not think that I had a problem like the rest of the folks in that place did and felt very inconvenienced by the whole thing. Quite a few treatment centers and many years of sobriety later, it's much easier to see their benefit. However, I do clearly see what the Con's are in committing to these institutions. Here are a few:

### Con's of Going to Treatment

**Time** - Yes, you are committing a substantial amount of your time to this program. You are committing literally ALL of your time if you elect to go to an inpatient treatment center. This means that family and work responsibilities need to be re-arranged. In many cases, some or all of those have "dissolved" on their own because of our drinking and drugging activities.

**Cost** - Most people would agree that this is the biggest downside to treatment, particularly private rehabs. Inpatient programs can cost upwards of $1,000 per day and outpatient programs are not cheap either. Publicly funded programs are more affordable but there are oftentimes many hoops to jump through to qualify and get into these programs.

### Pro's of Going to Treatment

**Structured Environment** - One of the biggest benefits of attending treatment, primarily residential (or inpatient), is that you are provided with a safe, structured environment that is free of distractions and temptations. This will give you a window of opportunity to get clean and sober (post-detox) and learn how to live life without drugs and alcohol. This structured environment is designed to essentially be free of the daily stressors of work, home and family so that you can focus only on your recovery.

**Establish Network of Positive People** - Attending treatment, inpatient or outpatient, gives you the opportunity to form new friendships and bonds with other like-minded, positive people. These are relationships that can be the beginning of your sober support network.

**Learning Better Holistic Health** - If giving up drinking and drugs were enough, this would be a much shorter book. However, the real purpose of recovery is to learn how to live a happy and healthy life without drugs and alcohol. Learning to treat yourself well in all respects in something that you can learn in treatment, such as eating right, being physically active and taking care of your mental and spiritual well-being.

**Save Money** - Wait, what?! Didn't we just say in the "Con's" that "cost" was a downside to going to treatment? Well, yes we did. BUT, let's look at the big picture here. The amount of money that you will save in long run by getting, and staying sober, is astounding compared to continuing with that financial minefield of active addiction. Many people are blown away when they see the financial figures tied to their disease. I'm not just talking about the money spent on drugs and alcohol (count this, though). Add in jobs lost, promotions lost, missed opportunities, legal fees, smashed cars, foreclosed homes, and so on. Looking at it this way, the cost of a stint at that fancy rehab may not look as outrageous as it did earlier.

**Save Your Life** - For some, it really does boil down to this. It's simply a matter of life or death. Without some real, structured help, the end is imminent. A lot of addicts and alcoholics run to treatment in hopes that they will "save" something or get their lives back. What many find is that they have been given an entirely new life that is infinitely better than anything they could have ever dreamed possible.

REHABILITATION

## Making the Most of Rehab If You Decide to Go

*...we do not always like what is good for us in this world. -Eleanor Roosevelt*

If you make the decision to go to a treatment facility, good for you! You are giving yourself a gift that will not only come back to you tenfold but to those you know and love as well, even if your relationships aren't as you would want them to be right now. As we reviewed earlier, there are so many different types of treatment facilities so it's not possible to give you a perfect run down of what to expect. However, here are a few words of wisdom so that you can make the most of your stay:

There will be no locks on the doors. This doesn't work, not even for a second, if you're not willing so you can walk away at any time. Even if you are court ordered to be at a place, they'll just come and pick you up to face your consequences at a later date should you bolt. Check your willingness level at the door, and thereafter frequently, and commit to stay for whatever term is recommended.

If you go - From my experience with the revolving doors of many treatment centers, these are my words of wisdom. First and foremost, check the attitude at the door. This is one thing that I took in with me and held onto through nearly all of my stays, except for the last one. It did me no favors. Thinking that I still knew what was best for me, after the shit storm that I had just made of my life was ludicrous. Also, demanding that I be given respect and attention when I felt I needed it was just as insane. I had to come to a place where I finally understood that I knew absolutely nothing about how to recover from this disease and that these people were clearly authorities on the subject. So probably, I should just let them do their job and listen to someone else for a change. Once I did this - made this mental shift (some would call it "surrender"), going to treatment was a blessing for me and I made the most of every single opportunity that was put in front of me to learn and to start my recovery. Yes, this included going to AA, which I also resisted for a long time.

## The Importance of Joining a Support Group

*Separate reeds are easily broken; but bound together they are strong and hard to break apart. -The Midrash*

Yes, we are talking about a 12 Step Group here, AA or NA preferably. There are alternative "recovery groups" out there but this author knows absolutely nothing about them or their success rates. What I do know is that 12 Step Groups work 100% for people that follow the directions 100%. That's the key. Many people, myself included, have avoided getting sober simply because they feared "joining" AA or NA. I had no concept of what this group was or just how something like this could possibly be of any assistance to me. I didn't understand what AA was and there is always the fear of the unknown.

So, what is AA then? What it is, really, is a multi-faceted program that incorporates meetings, fellowship and working a 12-step program in order to bring about a change in the alcoholic and provide continued growth and support. (NA is the same - they just change some words around in the "steps" and the literature is different.) AA was founded in 1935 by Bill Wilson (known as Bill W) and Dr. Robert Smith (known as Dr. Bob), based on the main principle of one alcoholic sharing their experiences with another. Within 4 years, their basic text called "Alcoholics Anonymous" (aka The Big Book) was published and membership blossomed. Today, there are over 2 million members of AA world-wide (over 1/2 of these in the U.S.) and over 115,000 registered AA Groups. In fact, there are now over 200 different fellowships that employ the "12 Steps" for recovery from AA (altered to fit). Hard to argue with those numbers.

Giving up control is difficult and joining a "Support Group" of any sort is giving up another layer of control with respect to this disease. Believe me - I get it. I had to get to a place in my life and with my disease where I finally understood that my way wasn't working in any way, shape or form and I became willing to try something else. Recovery from addiction happens on many levels: physical, mental, emotional and spiritual. The program of AA addresses these different levels of recovery through it's different facets of: attending meetings, getting a sponsor, working the 12 steps, spiritual principles and involvement in the fellowship. In doing these things, old habits are broken, new (healthy) habits are formed, and we are able to take a deeper look at the causes and conditions underlying our long drinking and using careers. All of this is done in some manner that taps into the mechanisms that counter the complex neurological and psychological processes through which this disease wreaks its havoc. Better yet, it's done through the power of "the group". Psychologists have long known that one of the best ways to change human behavior is to gather people with similar problems into groups instead of treating them individually. This is one of AA's precepts.

Whether it is the initial act of "surrender", the group support setting, the self-awareness that comes from working the Steps, or the close relationships in the fellowship through helping others that are the key components to the alcoholic's recovery (one or all of these), no one knows. What we do know, however, is that despite all we've learned over the past few decades about psychology, neurology, and human behavior, contemporary medicine has yet to devise anything that works markedly better. "In my 20 years of treating addicts, I've never seen anything else that comes close to the 12 steps," says Drew Pinsky, the addiction-medicine specialist who hosts VH1's Celebrity Rehab. While AA may not be a miracle cure for all, people who become deeply involved in the program stay sober and do well over the long haul, and this starts with attending meetings. Check out the Resources Section at the end of the book for links to various 12 Step Groups. It starts by attendance at the first meeting and goes from there. Addiction is not something that can, or should, be battled alone.

*"The feeling of having shared in a common peril is one element in the powerful cement which binds us." — Alcoholics Anonymous*

Road To
Recovery

# Recovery Resources

## Treatment Centers

There are no "public" websites that offer treatment center, detox and sober living directories. Unfortunately, any site you find will be filled with "sponsored results". This means rehabs that have paid for ad space. That's not always a bad thing, just not an unbiased thing. The best site I've found is Sober.com. You'll get the sponsored results in your search but you will also get all of the public listings as well, including the government-funded (some free) facilities.

## Support Groups

Alcoholics Anonymous (http://aa.org/)
Al-Anon Websites (http://www.al-anon.alateen.org/)
Narcotics Anonymous (http://www.na.org/)
Cocaine Anonymous (http://ca.org/)
Adult Children of Alcoholics (http://www.adultchildren.org/)
Co-Dependence Anonymous (CoDA) (http://www.coda.org/)

## Mental Health

National Institute of Mental Health (http://www.nimh.nih.gov/)
Results of biomedical research on mind and behavior.

National Alliance for the Mentally Ill (http://www.nami.org/)
Support for consumers with mental illness

Substance Abuse & Mental Health Services Administration
(http://www.samhsa.gov/)

United States Department of Health & Human Services

## Government Resources

Single-State Agency (SSA) Directory:
(http://www.recoverymonth.gov/Recovery-Month-Kit/Resources/Single-State-Agency-SSA-Directory.aspx)
Prevention and Treatment of Substance Use and Mental Disorders – A list of State offices that can provide local information and guidance about substance use and mental disorders, treatment, and recovery in your community.

AMVETS (http://www.amvets.org/)
This organization provides support for veterans and the active military in procuring their earned entitlements. It also offers community services that enhance the quality of life for this Nation's citizens.

## Professionals

Intervention Project for Nurses (http://www.ipnfl.org/)
Help for professionals with chemical dependencies.

International Lawyers in Alcoholics Anonymous (ILAA)
(http://www.ilaa.org/)
This organization serves as a clearinghouse for support groups for lawyers who are recovering from alcohol or other chemical dependencies.

International Pharmacists Anonymous (IPA)
(http://home.comcast.net/~mitchfields/ipa/ipapage.htm)
This is a 12-step fellowship of pharmacists and pharmacy students recovering from any addiction.

## Other

AlcoholScreening.org - Website offering an online screening tool to assess drinking patterns. The website offers visitors free confidential online screenings to assess their drinking patterns, giving them personalized feedback and showing them if their alcohol consumption is likely to be within safe limits. AlcoholScreening.org was developed by Join Together, a project of the Boston University School of Public Health, and was launched in April 2001. The website also provides answers to frequently asked questions about alcohol and health consequences, and provides links to support resources and a database of local treatment programs. Disclaimer: This site does not provide a diagnosis of alcohol abuse, alcohol dependence or any other medical condition. The information provided here cannot substitute for a full evaluation by a health professional, and should only be used as a guide to understanding your alcohol use and potential health issues.

This Center for Substance Abuse Prevention widget includes a variety of updates on activities relating to underage drinking which is updated regularly with local, state, and national articles published by online sources. (http://www.samhsa.gov/about/csap.aspx)

NCADD: (http://ncadd.org/) The National Council on Alcoholism and Drug Dependence, Inc. (NCADD) and its Affiliate Network is a voluntary health organization dedicated to fighting the Nation's #1 health problem – alcoholism, drug addiction and the devastating consequences of alcohol and other drugs on individuals, families and communities.

American Council for Drug Education (http://www.acde.org/) Educational programs and services for teens, parents, and educators

# About the Author

Taite Adams grew up everywhere. The only child of an Air Force navigator and school teacher, moving around became second nature by grade school. By age 20, she was an alcoholic, drug addict and self-proclaimed egomaniac. Pain is a great motivator, as is jail, and she eventually got sober has found peace and joy in this life beyond measure.

At the age of 42, Taite published her first book titled "Kickstart Your Recovery". Now permanently Free on Amazon, the book answers many of the questions that she herself had but was afraid to ask before giving up the fight with addiction and entering recovery over a decade prior. Since, she has published four other recovery books, including her bestselling book on Opiate Addiction, and has moved into the broader spirituality and self-help genres.

Leading a spiritual life is all about choices. The practice of spiritual principles and the willingness to remain teachable are the key ingredients for growth. As a spiritual seeker and reader of the self-help genre herself, Taite appreciates and respects each and every person who takes the time to read her works and respond with reviews and comments. For more information on books, upcoming releases, and to connect with the author, go to http://www.taiteadams.com.

**Check out our active Facebook Page: Taite Adams Recovery Books (https://www.facebook.com/TaiteAdams).**

As you begin your Road to Recovery, please check out Taite's first book, Kickstart Your Recovery, available in both Kindle (where's it is Permanently FREE) and Paperback.

Opiate Addiction has reached epidemic proportions in this country and is something that Taite is intimately familiar with. Read her bestselling book on this topic, chronicling this insidious killer and laying the pathway for freedom from its grip.

If you or a loved one are in recovery from alcoholism or addiction and want to learn more about emotional sobriety, check out Taite's book titled Restart Your Recovery, also on Amazon.com.

It's hard to miss mention in the media of the drug Molly and the controversy surrounding it's use and it's ingredients. There is plenty of confusion there as well. Check out Taite's latest book, called Who is Molly? for the latest info on this drug and it's dangers.

Have you ever wanted to learn more about Ego? Taite's latest book, titled E-Go: Ego Distancing Through Mindfulness, Emotional Intelligence & The Language of Love, takes an in depth look at ego. Consider how you define yourself and how to live a happier life, apart from ego in your career, relationships, and health.

Kickstart Your Recovery
The Road Less Traveled to
Freedom from Addiction
Taite Adams

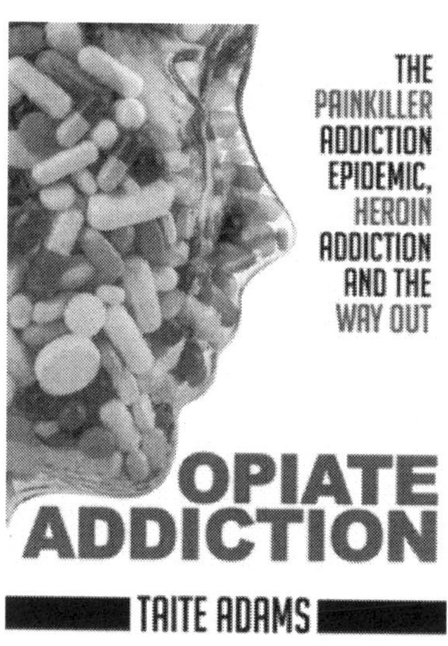
THE
PAINKILLER
ADDICTION
EPIDEMIC,
HEROIN
ADDICTION
AND THE
WAY OUT
OPIATE
ADDICTION
TAITE ADAMS

RESTART
YOUR
RECOVERY
12 Things You Can Do
To Get Back On The Beam
TAITE ADAMS

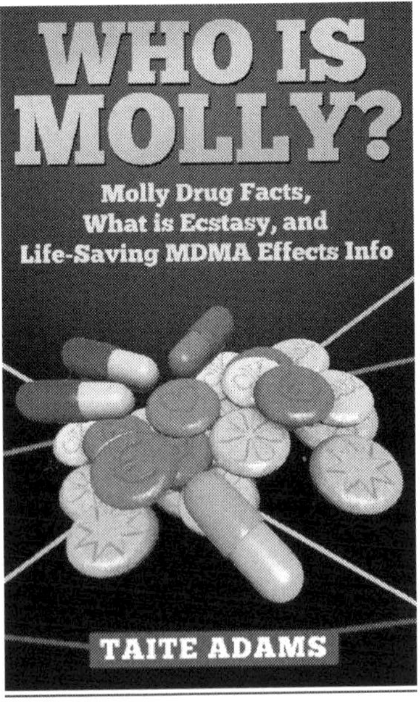
WHO IS
MOLLY?
Molly Drug Facts,
What is Ecstasy, and
Life-Saving MDMA Effects Info
TAITE ADAMS

E-GO
Ego Distancing Through Mindfulness, Emotional Intelligence and the Language of Love
TAITE ADAMS

Printed in Great Britain
by Amazon